CONTENT-BASED VIDEO RETRIEVAL

A Database Perspective

THE KLUWER INTERNATIONAL SERIES
IN ENGINEERING AND COMPUTER SCIENCE

CONTENT-BASED VIDEO RETRIEVAL

A Database Perspective

by

Milan Petković
University of Twente, The Netherlands

Willem Jonker
University of Twente and Philips Research, The Netherlands

SPRINGER SCIENCE+BUSINESS MEDIA, LLC

Library of Congress Cataloging-in-Publication

Title: ***CONTENT-BASED VIDEO RETRIEVAL: A Database Perspective***

Author: Milan Petković and Willem Jonker
ISBN 978-1-4419-5396-4 ISBN 978-1-4757-4865-9 (eBook)
DOI 10.1007/978-1-4757-4865-9

Printed on acid-free paper.

Contents

Foreword

The area of content-based video retrieval is a very hot area both for research and for commercial applications. In order to design effective video databases for applications such as digital libraries, video production, and a variety of Internet applications, there is a great need to develop effective techniques for content-based video retrieval. One of the main issues in this area of research is how to bridge the semantic gap between low-level features extracted from a video (such as color, texture, shape, motion, and others) and semantics that describe video concept on a higher level. In this book, Dr. Milan Petković and Prof. Dr. Willem Jonker have addressed this issue by developing and describing several innovative techniques to bridge the semantic gap.

The main contribution of their research, which is the core of the book, is the development of three techniques for bridging the semantic gap: (1) a technique that uses the spatio-temporal extension of the Cobra framework, (2) a technique based on hidden Markov models, and (3) a technique based on Bayesian belief networks. To evaluate performance of these techniques, the authors have conducted a number of experiments using real video data. The book also discusses domains solutions versus general solution of the problem. Petković and Jonker proposed a solution that allows a system to be applied in multiple domains with minimal adjustments. They also designed and described a prototype video database management system, which is based on techniques they proposed in the book.

Borko Furht
Boca Raton, Florida
June 2003

Preface

Recent advances in computing, communication, and data storage have led to an increasing number of large digital libraries that are becoming publicly available on the Internet. In addition to alphanumeric data, other modalities like video are starting to play an important role in these libraries. As video is quite voluminous, it turns out to be very difficult to find required information in the enormous mass of data stored in a library. Ordinary retrieval techniques are not appropriate for a practical usage of digital video libraries, because of the obvious difference in the nature of the documents in video on the one hand, and text collections on the other hand. Instead of words, a video retrieval system deals with collections of video records. Therefore, the system is confronted with the problem of video understanding. It has to gather key information about a video in order to allow users to query semantics instead of the raw video data or video features. Users expect tools that automatically understand and manipulate the video content in the same structured way as a traditional database manages numeric and textual data. Consequently, content-based search and retrieval of video data becomes a challenging and important problem.

This book focuses particularly on the topic of content-based video retrieval. After addressing basic concepts and techniques in the field, it concentrates on the semantic gap problem, i.e. the problem of inferring semantics from raw video data, as the main problem of content-based video retrieval. The book identifies and proposes the integrated use of three different techniques to bridge the semantic gap, namely, spatio-temporal formalization methods, hidden Markov models, and dynamic Bayesian networks. As the problem is approached from a database perspective, the emphasis is put on evolving from a database management system into a video database management system that allows a user to retrieve the desired video sequence among huge amounts of video data in an efficient and semantically meaningful way. With respect to that, the book also presents a modeling framework and a prototype of a content-based video management system that integrates the three methods and provides efficient, flexible, and scalable content-based video retrieval. The proposed approach is validated in the domain of sport videos for which some experimental results are presented.

The material presented in this book is a selection from the PhD dissertation of the first author under supervision of the second author.

Milan Petković & Willem Jonker

Acknowledgments

We wish to acknowledge all the people who have helped us in the completion of this book. First of all, we would like to thank Borko Furht for taking the initiative of publishing our work in this series, as well as Susan-Lagerstrom-Fife and Jennifer Evans from Kluwer Academic Publishers for supporting it. We are indebted to Vojkan Mihajlović for his contribution to the Formula 1 case study. We also would like to thank Zoran Živković for the joint work on the processing of tennis videos, and Roelof van Zwol and Menzo Windhouwer for the good cooperation in the DMW demo. Many others contributed, in particular, Nevenka Dimitrova, Peter Apers, Dejan and Tanja Mitrović, Djoerd Hiemstra, and Violeta Milenković. Finally, and most importantly, we would like to thank our families for their support, patience, and understanding.

Chapter 1

INTRODUCTION

1. MOTIVATION

It is expected that a number of large digital video libraries (see for example [1-3]) will become publicly available in the near future, as a result of recent developments in digital video technology, the Internet, and computer performance. The production of video information turned out to be low-priced and open to everyone. Huge amounts of audio-visual data are produced everyday from surveillance cameras, TV programs, and home video cameras. On the other hand, the advances in digital storage technology, which doubles storage capacity every year, make digitization, compression, archiving, and streaming of video data popular and inexpensive. Finally, the expansions of the Internet and technologies that support the broadband access, such as xDSL[1], have provided means for the widespread distribution and the usage of video and other multimedia data. Some TV broadcasters [2-4] already offer the digital streams of their programs through the Internet, and a lot of events are covered by video in real-time on the Internet. It is expected that the trend of rapid growth of audio-visual data will continue in the future, following the progression of the digital television technology and possible integration of TV and Web. Consequently, the number of digital libraries will grow, as well as the number of hours of video recordings they accumulate.

However, large amounts of data and its audio-visual nature put quit a number of challenges in front of systems that manipulate this data. Problems

[1] xDSL represents a number of technologies under the DSL umbrella. DSL stands for Digital Subscriber Line.

are especially encountered with respect to the retrieval of the audio-visual data. Ordinary retrieval techniques are not appropriate for a practical usage within digital video libraries. The high volume of audio-visual content makes free browsing almost impossible. It is tedious and time-consuming for a user to browse through a big collection of video footage and find the desired information. Moreover, this process becomes much worse if a user wants to find only a specific part of a specific video in these big video collections. In that case, the process includes searching for a video and then viewing the entire video to find the desired part. Still, the retrieval process can rely on textual annotation of audio-visual information, which is added as metadata manually or using (semi-) automatic tools during the cataloguing process. The annotations (metadata) can be used for retrieval as it is done by the multimedia search engine of Lycos [5] or AltaVista video search [6]. However, annotation-based search has several limitations. The cataloguing phase, which is often done manually, requires considerable amount of human resources to annotate every video clip. Furthermore, the text associated with video fragments is often vague and incomplete due to subjective human perception of the audio-visual content.

The inefficiency and limitations of traditional retrieval approaches have resulted in a demand for new techniques that can manipulate the video data based on its content. Content-based retrieval has been identified as one of most challenging problems, requiring a multidisciplinary research among information retrieval, databases, computer vision, digital signal processing, artificial intelligence, pattern recognition, psychology, and other fields. Each of these fields provides necessary building blocks for a content-based retrieval system. For example, a content-based retrieval system must have the ability to efficiently store and retrieve multimedia documents in the same way as a database management system does with alphanumerical data. As video data is different from alphanumeric data (multiple modalities, ambiguity of interpretation, voluminous nature, etc.), it is far more difficult to interpret a video document than an alphanumeric one. A content-based retrieval system has to be capable to process a digital video signal and extract specific low-level features from this signal. To understand the video content, the system has to derive the semantics from the video data using the achievements of artificial intelligence, computer vision, and pattern recognition fields. The system has to be aware of human psychology. It has to understand how the human perception system works, and use this knowledge for computer vision and user interaction purposes.

2. VIDEO RETRIEVAL FROM A DATA MANAGEMENT PERSPECTIVE

It has been explained in the previous section that the solution to the content-based video retrieval problem lies at the crossroads among many fields and cannot be completely solved by any of these participating disciplines alone. It requires a combination of information retrieval, database, and computer vision among other technologies. Bearing in mind the drawbacks of current video retrieval systems that will be surveyed in chapters 2 and 3, and, on the other hand, successful applications of database systems in manipulating structured data, as well as scalability, extensibility, and generality of the approach, we choose databases as our starting point.

The database technologies allow a large amount of alphanumeric data to be stored and retrieved in an efficient way. They define the exact mappings from conceptual models, which are close to the user perspective of data, to physical data models, which are used by the system to manage the data. For example, in a relational system, the Entity-Relationship model is translated into a relational model where the data is organized into tables. Consequently a user query, which is defined in SQL, is transformed through the relational algebra into operations over the physical implementation of the data representation. However, this ideal picture changes when new types of data, which are much more complex than alphanumeric data, such as video data, are brought into the database environment. It has been shown that a traditional database management system does not provide proper facilities for managing and retrieving video data [7, 8]. Video data requires different data models, which have to capture various types of information from different modalities involved in a video document. A video model should represent the content of these modalities together with their structure. Consequently, a video management system has to provide means for bridging the big gap between such a video model, which is close to human perception of video, and a series of pixels, which is the physical representation of video on the disk. In addition, the system must facilitate a quite different kind of query processing. In contrast to the traditional one, it involves similarity search, query by example, browsing, and most importantly content-based retrieval.

In the light of that, ***the aim of the work presented in this book is to investigate what techniques are necessary to be added to a database management system to support content based video retrieval.*** From the database perspective, the question is how a database management system should evolve into a video database management system that allows a user to retrieve the desired video sequence among huge amounts of video data in a quick, efficient, and semantically meaningful way.

As the mentioned research topic is very broad, requiring expertise in different fields mentioned above, we concentrate on some specific aspects of the research topic. The book focuses on the semantic gap problem, i.e. the problem of inferring semantics from raw video data, as the main problem of content-based video retrieval. In addition, we consider some particular issues that arise after approaching the main problem from the database perspective. First, video modeling issues have to be addressed, as a prerequisite to the database support for content-based video retrieval. Next, some system issues, such as architecture, system implementation and query processing issues need to be considered to achieve the main goal. The following sections explain further the main requirements a database management system has to accomplish to support content-based video retrieval.

2.1 Video modeling

It is recognized by the database research community [7, 8] that video data requires a new data model that is different from the traditional data model. While the traditional data model deals only with data structure, the video data model has to include, except the elements that represent video structure, also the elements that represent the content of video data. A video data model should be able to capture and represent various types of information about multimedia objects and provide a sophisticated representation of video content in terms of low-level features, but also high-level concepts. Given the importance of different video representations, which is not reflected in the state of the art video retrieval systems, the first goal of the research presented in this book is to identify a video modeling framework that combines low and high level representation of video content and provides support for content-based video retrieval. In addition, we investigate if this framework can be used to model video data in such a way that it is independent of techniques used for content extraction, as well as of an application domain.

2.2 Bridging the semantic gap

The early content-based video retrieval techniques index the video data based on its audio and visual content, such as color, textures, and motion, among others. The automatic computing of the low level features has been relatively quickly achieved. However, the low level features do not provide the semantics that describe video concepts on a higher level. And this is precisely what an average user has in mind while starting the retrieval process, a much more abstract notion than low level visual features. The main problem in content-based retrieval is how to bridge this gap between low-level features and semantics. This book addresses the semantic gap problem and provides the answers to related questions, such as: What are the techniques that are able to deal with automatic concept extraction based on low-level features? Can we validate such a technique in a specific application domain? Can these techniques support multi-modalities to improve retrieval results?

2.3 System architecture and implementation

The next objective of this book is to investigate specific issues regarding the architecture and implementation of a video retrieval system. Given our starting point, we discuss the integration of the techniques, which are used to extract the video content, within a database management system. We pay special attention on the support for dynamic feature/semantics extraction.

Many researchers agree that the near future will not bring a general solution for the problem of semantic gap. As it will be shown in this book a feasible solution is a domain dependent approach that uses domain knowledge to close the gap between the low-level video features and high-level representation of video content. It is expected that a number of approaches developed for particular domains will provide a solution for these domains and help in solving the main problem. Bearing this in mind, we discuss the architecture of a content-based retrieval system that minimizes the necessary adjustment of the system when the application domain changes.

3. RESEARCH APPROACH

In this section, we briefly describe our approach to the content-based video retrieval problem by addressing the three main topics identified above.

To address the issues regarding video modeling we survey the existing video models and discuss their advantages and drawbacks. Next, we propose an approach that overcome the identified shortcomings and develop a modeling framework called Cobra. The framework is developed to facilitate validation of our ideas regarding video modeling and to support the integration of low-level and high-level representation of video content. An additional goal is to provide the basis for the system that can be used to validate different methods for interpreting raw data into semantic content. Furthermore, we extend the framework with spatio-temporal and the other necessary operators needed to support spatio-temporal formalization of video objects and events.

By introducing the spatio-temporal extension of the framework, we identify at the same time the first method to bridge the semantic gap. The other two techniques, which we use to deal with the semantic gap problem, are hidden Markov models, and Bayesian belief networks. The applicability of these three techniques for content derivation is validated using the Cobra framework and two case studies. For each case study, we introduce video processing and feature extraction schemes that operate on real video data. To evaluate the retrieval performance, a number of experiments are carried out that measure the performance in terms of precision and recall. Moreover, we experimentally compare the retrieval performance of the system when it uses only one modality, with its performance when multimodal information sources are used.

With the aim of addressing the system architecture and implementation issues, we propose a design of a content-based video retrieval system. In order to be able to integrate the techniques used for content extraction in an efficient and flexible manner, we choose for an extensible database platform. The proposed methods are implemented within a prototype of a video database management system extending the database platform at all three levels of the traditional ANSI/SPARC architecture [9]. The obtained prototype is applied in different domains in order to investigate to what extent it can be functional and what are the necessary adjustments. Some video processing and feature/semantics extraction techniques are integrated within the prototype aiming at the analysis of the feasibility and effectiveness of the incremental and dynamical change of metadata.

4. OUTLINE OF THE BOOK

This book is organized as follows:

Chapter 2: Database management systems and content-based retrieval

This chapter presents basic concepts of database management systems. It also introduces an experimental database management system that is used as the basis for the prototype of a video database management system presented in Chapter 6 of this book. Then, the chapter moves the reader's attention from databases via information retrieval to content-based video retrieval, which is the main subject of the book. The chapter also explains the nature of video data, gives some fundamentals of content-based retrieval, and briefly describes the MPEG-7 standard.

Chapter 3: Video modeling

Chapter 3 deals with video modeling. It discusses differences between multimedia modeling and traditional data modeling taking into account the requirements for content-based retrieval. In particular, a difference is made between the modeling of the video structure and the modeling of the video content. The chapter surveys the existing approaches for both topics. Next, the chapter discusses the shortcomings of surveyed models and introduces a video modeling framework called Cobra that aims at integrating the low-level feature representation and the high level semantic representation of video content. Finally, the chapter introduces the first of two case studies that are described in the book. The Tennis case study is used in the chapter to demonstrate the parsing of video data into basic units, as well as their classification into some meaningful groups.

Chapter 4: Spatio-temporal formalization of video events

This chapter elaborates on the Cobra framework introducing an extension of the framework that supports spatio-temporal formalization of video events. The extension is used for the extraction of semantic concepts, such as video objects and events, which is demonstrated using the Tennis case study. After parsing and classification of the video records of tennis matches, which is described in Chapter 3, in this chapter the focus is moved to the automatic extraction of events like net-playing, rally, lob, etc.

Chapter 5: Stochastic modeling of video events

To overcome the limitations of the spatio-temporal approach, this chapter introduces two stochastic techniques for the modeling of video content. It demonstrates how they can be successfully used for content-based retrieval. The chapter starts with a brief description of the basic principles of Hidden Markov Models (HMMs) and Bayesian networks. The remainder of the chapter illustrates the application of these techniques on real video data through two case studies. In the Tennis case study, HMMs are applied for the recognition of different tennis strokes. The chapter describes a number of experiments with HMMs that are carried out in order to find which combination of features gives the best results for stroke recognition. The second case study deals with the video footage from Formula 1 races. This case study investigates the applicability of Bayesian networks for extracting Formula 1 highlights. The chapter introduces feature and text extraction schemes for the audio-visual analysis of that particular domain. In addition, this case study examines the effectiveness of multimodal retrieval compared to the retrieval process that uses only one modality.

Chapter 6: Cobra: A prototype of a video DBMS

This chapter introduces the prototype of a video database management system that implements the most ideas presented throughout this book. The chapter starts with a proposal of an architecture for content-based video retrieval system. Furthermore, the chapter describes the implementation platform that the system is built on. It illustrates how a database management system can be extended to support feature extraction and the methods for semantics extraction presented in chapters 4 and 5. The chapter shows how these different techniques can be used in an integrated way. Finally, the chapter describes the integration of content-based video retrieval and the concept-based search.

Chapter 7: Conclusions

The final chapter summarizes the book and brings conclusions with respect to the research questions posed in Section 2. It points out the contributions of the research described in the book and indicates some directions for future research.

5. MAIN CONTRIBUTIONS

Original contributions of the work presented in this book span the areas of content-based video retrieval. In particular, two major contributions can be summarized as follows:

- Closing the semantic gap in restricted domains by the integrated use of the spatio-tempoal approach, HMMs, and dynamic Bayesian networks, and
- Integration of these technologies within a DBMS, which (1) allows the system to be used in multiple domains with minimal adjustments and (2) provides a user with dynamic feature and semantics extraction.

REFERENCES

[1] The Library of Congress, Digital Collection and Programs, http://www.loc.gov/library/libarch-digital.html

[2] Cable News Network LP, CNN Video, http://europe.cnn.com/video/

[3] British Broadcasting Corporation, BBC Video Nation, http://www.bbc.co.uk/videonation/

[4] British Broadcasting Corporation, BBC World, http://www.bbcworld.com/

[5] Lycos, Carnegie Mellon University, Multimedia Search, http://multimedia.lycos.com

[6] AltaVista, AltaVista Search: Video Search, http://www.altavista.com/sites/search/svideo

[7] A. Yoshitaka, T. Ichikawa, "A Survey on Content-Based Retrieval for Multimedia Databases", *IEEE Transactions on Knowledge and Data Engineering*, 11(1), 1999, pp. 81-93.

[8] W. Grosky, "Managing Multimedia Information in Database Systems", *Communications of the ACM*, Vol. 40, No. 12, Dec. 1997, pp. 73-80.

[9] D. Tsichritzis, A. Klug, editors, "The ANSI/X3/SPARC DBMS Framework", *AFIPS Press*, 1978.

[10] R.Bayer, E.M. McCreight, "Organization and Maintenance of Large Ordered Indices", *Acta Informatica*, 1(3), 1972, pp.173-189.

Chapter 2

DATABASE MANAGEMENT SYSTEMS AND CONETENT-BASED RETRIEVAL

1. INTRODUCTION

Database management systems have been extensively used for more than 30 years as a standard tool for manipulating large amounts of alphanumeric data. They allow efficient and fast access to stored data taking the advantage of the fact that data is structured. With the emergence of the Web, large volumes of unstructured data have become available. As database management systems were not capable of storing and searching that data efficiently, information retrieval systems took over, providing search methods for unstructured textual documents. However, with further emergence of the Web and multimedia the importance of systems that can manage and search audio-visual data has arisen.

This chapter provides an introduction to databases, information retrieval, and content-based video retrieval. The next section presents fundamental concepts of database management systems. It discusses issues related to the database architecture and reviews the most prevalent data models. In this section, we also introduce an example of a database management system, which provides the basis for the implementation of a prototype of a content-based video retrieval system (described in Chapter 6). In Section 3, we present some basic concepts of information retrieval and define measures, which are used to characterize performance of our retrieval strategies in Chapter 5. Section 4 explains the nature of video data and introduces fundamentals of content-based video retrieval. It also surveys different methods for searching video data, as well as the MPEG-7 standard. Finally, Section 5 summarizes the chapter.

2. DATABASES

In this section, we review the fundamentals of database management systems. The section is meant to serve as an introduction and the basis for Chapter 6 of this book, where we describe a database management system that is extended to support content-based video retrieval. Therefore, after revisiting basic database concepts, a universal database architecture, and essential data models used by database management systems, we introduce the Moa-Monet database management system that functions as an implementation platform for the research presented in this book.

2.1 Database fundamentals

In our information society the word database is very common, representing an important aspect of business, engineering, and library science among other fields. Elmasri and Navathe [1] defined a database as a collection of related data, i.e. facts that can be recorded and that have implicit meaning. Databases model some aspects of the real world. However, they are intended to be used for a specific purpose by a group of users and applications. For example, consider the filmography of a video club that contains movie titles, director and actor names, and years of production, among other data. This data can be used to help members of the video club to find a movie that they like to rent. The data can be kept in book catalogues, but also using a software system, called the database management system (DBMS), which allows databases to be defined, constructed, and manipulated.

A DBMS facilitates specifying the data types and structures, insertion and storing the data on some medium controlled by the system, updating, and querying the data. For example, for our movie database, we should specify elements that describe a movie (for instance, title, release date, director, and editor), an actor/actress, a video club member, etc. Consequently, a data type for each data element has to be defined. Furthermore, relationships among data (for example between actors and movies) have to be taken into account. After constructing the database, the data can be queried and updated. An example query could be "Retrieve all movies directed by George Lucas". However, this informal query must be specified precisely in the query language understood by the DBMS.

One can think of developing a simple program that will work with files to achieve similar functionality as of our movie database. Elmasri and Navathe defined four main characteristics that distinguish the database approach from the file-processing approach: (1) self-describing nature of database, (2) insulation between programs and data and data abstraction, (3) support of multiple views of the data, and (4) sharing of data among multiple transactions.

The major characteristic of a database system is that it contains a complete definition of data structure and constraints. In the traditional file processing approach, this is typically the responsibility of the program, while a DBMS stores this metadata in the system catalog, providing a general purpose of the system. Therefore, the same system can be used for our movie data collection, but also for company administration data, for example.

Next, the database approach assures insulation between programs and data. If the structures of data change (for example, we add the number of rentals to the movie description), the programs that access this data are not influenced. The only thing that has to be changed is the metadata (definition) in the catalog, because this is the data about data that is used by the DBMS programs when they manipulate the data. On the other hand, in traditional file processing, if the structures of data change the programs that access data have to be changed, since they embed the structures of data files. The database approach offers a conceptual representation of the data, hiding the storage details from users. This is achieved by introducing a schema, which stores the description of a database in a specific data model used by the system.

As a database usually has many users that see the database from different perspectives, a DBMS supports multiple views of the data. Each view can contain a subset of the database and also some data that is derived from the database but not stored. For example, the owner of a video club might be interested in the movie titles of his movie database and the total number of rentals.

A DBMS has a property that it provides sharing the data among multiple users that can access the database at a time. To ensure consistency and accuracy, the system has to include concurrency control. This eliminates the possibility that in our example of the video club database two members reserve the same copy of a movie for the same day.

2.2 DBMS architecture

To further clarify the main database concepts, let us examine an architecture for database systems, called the three-schema architecture, which is proposed by ANSI/SPARC[1] study group in 1975 [2]. This architecture has been widely adopted as a standard model for the database architecture. It helps to achieve and visualize program-data independence, data abstraction, support for multiple user views and existence of a catalog.

The architecture is illustrated in Figure 2.1. As its name says, the architecture recognizes three different levels in a database system: internal, conceptual, and external level.

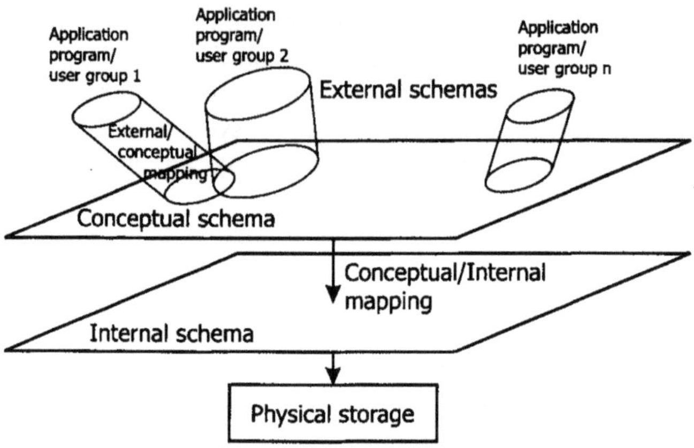

Figure 2.1. The three-level architecture

The internal level provides a low-level representation of the entire database. It has an internal schema that uses a physical data model to describe how the data is stored in the database. The internal schema is concerned with storage details, such as definition of various record types, representation of stored files, indices, etc. However, below the internal level, the architecture assumes a physical level, which is managed by the operating system, so the internal schema does not deal with device specific issues, such as cylinder or track sizes.

The conceptual level has a conceptual schema, which is a representation of the structure of the whole database. This schema describes the stored data and the existing relationships among the data, but hides the storage details.

The external level is the level at which users interact with the database via application programs or a language. This level includes a number of schemas. Each schema describes a part of the database that is relevant to a particular user group and hides the rest of the database (user views). Some views can have some derived or calculated data that is not actually stored in the database.

[1] American National Standard Institute/Standards Planning and Requirements Committee

The three schemas provide different descriptions of data, which is actually stored at the physical level. In order to manipulate data, a user request that is specified on an external level has to be transformed through conceptual level into a request on the internal schema. Hence, there are two levels of mapping in the architecture: conceptual/internal mapping and external/conceptual mapping.

As a result, users can access the same data, but have a different customized view of the data. They do not deal directly with physical database storage details. If the storage structures change, their views are not affected. If the physical aspects of the storage change, internal structure of the database should not be affected. In this way, the architecture provides logical and physical data independence.

2.3 Data models

As already mentioned, a data model helps in providing a user with a set of concepts that are used to describe the structure of a database, ensuring data abstraction. The presented architecture distinguishes among three types of data models: conceptual, implementation, and physical data models.

Conceptual data models provide concepts that are close to the user perception of data. A well-known example is the Entity-Relationship (ER) model. The concepts it uses are entities, attributes, and relationships. An entity represents an object with a real or conceptual existence in the world, such as movie or actor in our example. Attributes represent some properties of entities, like the title or release date of the movie. Relationships characterize associations among the entities, such as 'acts' relationship between an actor and a movie (Shannon Elizabeth acts in American Pie). An example of the ER model of a part of our movie database is depicted in Figure 2.2.

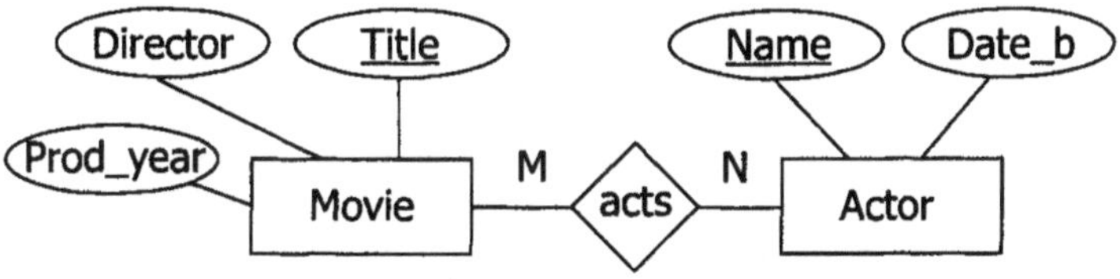

Figure 2.2. ER model of the movie database

Physical data models provide low-level concepts that describe details of how is data stored in the computer system, such as record formats, orderings, and access paths.

Implementation data models are at the level between two previously described classes. They represent concepts that might be understood by the users of a database system, but which are close to the representation used within a computer system. There are three typical implementation models: hierarchical, network, and relational. Each uses a record structure to represent data. The network and hierarchical models, which are based on traversing data links to process a database, have been used in the past.

The development of the relational data model [3] was a huge step forward in the database field. Nowadays, relational database management systems that are based on the relational data model are widely used. The relational data model represents data as a collection of relations. Each relation can be depicted as a table where columns represent attributes and rows (tuples) represent entities.

The relational data model has a strong mathematical foundation. To define it, we need to introduce some concepts: A domain is a finite set of values. The Cartesian product of domains $D_1, D_2, \ldots, D_n$, written as $D_1 \times D_2 \times \ldots \times D_n$ is set of all tuples $(x_1, x_2, \ldots, x_n)$ such that $\forall$ i, (i = 1, 2, ..., n), $x_i \in D_i$. A relation is any subset of the Cartesian product of one or more domains. The arity (degree) of a relation R, $R \subseteq D_1 \times D_2 \times \ldots \times D_n$ is n. Some tuples of a relation might not correspond to the valid set of data according to the intended semantics of the database. A set of constraints, that include domain constraints, key constraints, entity integrity, and referential integrity constraints, assure that data in the database have meaningful interpretations. The relational model of our movie database is presented in Figure 2.3.

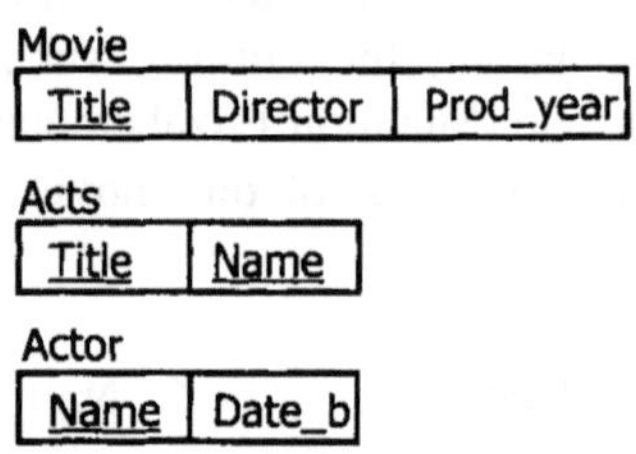

Figure 2.3. The relational model of the movie database

Current relational database management systems typically use SQL (Structured Query Language) to enable a user to create relations, insert, and query the data. Usually this language is used for data and view definition, as well as for data manipulation. For example, a query that selects all movies directed by George Lucas, returning only titles and production years would be formulated as follows:

```
SELECT Title, Prod_year FROM Movie WHERE Director ='George Lucas';
```

More details about the relational data model, relation algebra, and SQL can be found in [1, 4].

Finally, we will mention object data models as implementation models that are closer to conceptual models. They are developed to overcome the shortcomings of relational, network, and hierarchical data models when dealing with complex applications, such as CAD/CAM, multimedia, and GIS among others. Another reason for the introduction of object models is the increasing use of object-oriented (OO) programming languages. The key concepts of the OO approach are encapsulation of operations, object persistence, and relationships that include inheritance, aggregation, and association. The object model is standardized within ODMG 2.0 [5]. More details about object models can be found in [1, 6]. In Figure 2.4, the reader can observe the difference between the relational and the object model of our movie database.

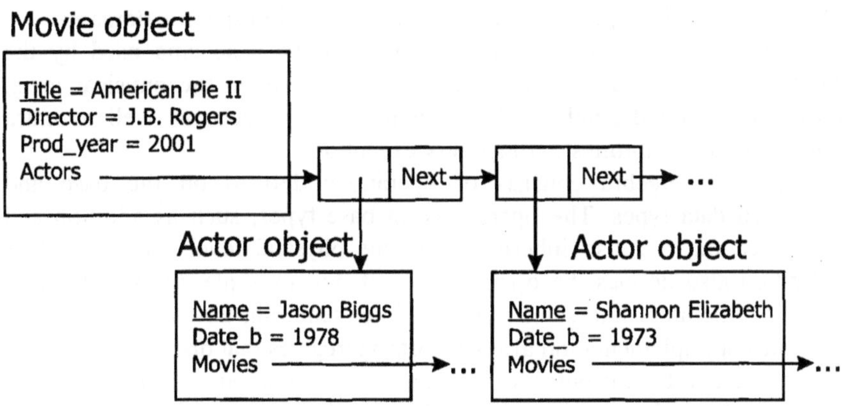

Figure 2.4. Differences between OO and relational concepts

Different approaches have been used to implement OO concepts into database management systems. However, most of them have indicated many problems with sharing data between applications, efficient query processing, and scalability. In the following subsection, we present a database architecture that was developed in order to investigate how a database management system can support structural object orientation in an efficient manner [7, 8].

2.4 The Moa-Monet database platform

Here we present a general architecture and the basic concepts of a database management system, which extension to the system that supports content-based retrieval will be explained in Chapter 6. Instead of transforming object queries directly into operations in physical algebra, the system provides a structural object-oriented data model and algebra which is mapped onto a binary relational model. This mapping is performed using the Moa framework [7]. The physical level data model used at the internal level is the binary relational data model provided by Monet [9].

Moa is an extensible framework that defines an object data model and algebra. Moa distinguishes between base types and structured types that are generated via a type constructor. The examples of base types are integer, real, character, etc. Moa accepts all base types of the underlying physical storage system and allows their orthogonal combination using the structure primitives set, tuple, and object. Structures can be used recursively.

Moa is extensible in various ways. If it is built on a system that provides base type extensibility, Moa inherits it, so the base types are also extensible. Furthermore, the data model and algebra are also extensible by defining new Moa structures and operations that can be beneficial in specific domains.

Available data structures are used to describe a schema used by the structural object-oriented model. They are mapped on the physical level, providing data independence between these two levels, as well as extra optimization possibilities during query execution.

The Moa algebra consists of operations defined on the base and structured data types. The operations on base types, such as addition and multiplication, are also inherited from the physical level. Each structure definition also defines the operations on it. For example, the set structure specifies operators like select, project, join, semijoin, union, intersect, etc. The current implementation also supports aggregates that operate on sets and allows access to attributes of tuples. Each operation is translated into efficient physical execution plan understood by the physical level (in this case using Monet Interface Language). More details about Moa can be found in [7]. The following example defines the Movie class and selects all movies directed by George Lucas, returning only titles and production years.

```
class Movie:
TUPLE<
Atomic<Mo_title>: Title,
Atomic<Mo_director>: Direcor,
Atomic<Mo_prod_year>: Prod_year,
SET<Mo_Ac_ind, OBJECT<Actor, Mo_Ac_ref>, Mo_ids>: Actors
>extension MovieExt;

map[TUPLE<%Title, %Prod_year]
(select[=(%Director,"George Lucas")](MovieExt));
```

At the physical level, the system uses Monet [9] – an extensible parallel database kernel that supports a binary relational model. The binary relational model is based on Binary Association Tables (BATs). They consists of two columns, each storing atomic values (often in the form of [oid, attribute] pairs). The structured data is vertically decomposed over narrow BATs, as it is shown in Figure 2.5 for the Movie class. The reason for vertical decomposition is to gain performance when dealing with applications that use only a few attributes of a relation in the query processing.

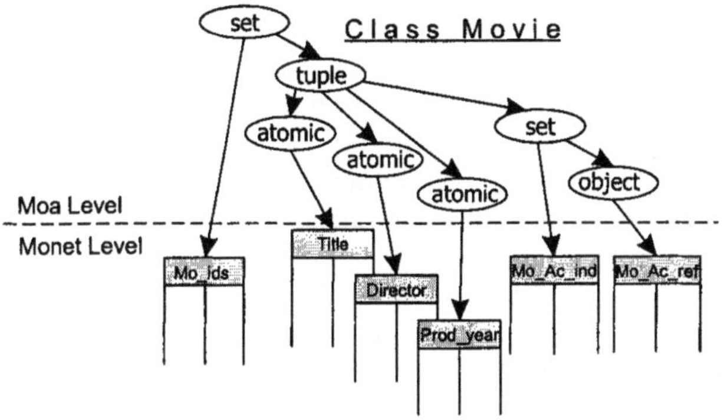

Figure 2.5. The BAT structure of the Movie class

Monet performs all operations in main memory assuming that the data fit there. For large databases it relies on virtual memory. Monet Interface Language offers a set of low level algebra operators, such as the set operations select and join. Based on the properties of the operands, Monet chooses the most efficient algorithm for the execution of an operation. In that way, the join of two ordered columns will be performed by a mergejoin, while if the join columns are identical, a syncjoin will be used. Extensibility with new atomic types, but also new search accelerators is achieved by extension modules. These modules have to be specified using Monet Extension Language (MEL).

Monet also supports parallel execution of algebraic operators. Parallelism is incorporated using parallel blocks in MIL (an example will be given in Chapter 6).

The database architecture presented above has been already used and extended for different applications, such as geographic information systems [10] and content-based image and text retrieval [8].

3. INFORMATION RETRIEVAL

Information retrieval is the academic discipline, which deals with the task of finding information items that are relevant to the information need. Since recently information retrieval systems have mainly concentrated on large amounts of textual information. However, with the growth of audiovisual information available in the digital format, multimedia retrieval has become an important field for research. This section will give some basic principles of information retrieval, providing an introduction to the more specific description of the content-based video retrieval, which will be given in the next section.

Typical examples of information retrieval systems are search engines that can be found on the web or in a library. They concentrate on finding text documents, performing full text retrieval. After a user types in several keywords, the system returns the documents that are most interesting according to the system.

To satisfy a user's information need, an information retrieval system typically addresses different technical issues. It deals with the representation of documents in the collection, as well as with the representation of user queries. Finally, it has to perform calculations using a retrieval strategy to retrieve appropriate documents.

Let us clarify this by an example. Assume that each movie in our video club database is associated with a text document that describes the movie. If a user specifies for instance 'comedy' as a keyword for his search, the system will retrieve a ranked list of documents. For example, the documents can be ranked based on the number of times the keyword appears in them. However, different strategies can be used for retrieval. Some of most often used models are the Boolean model, the vector space model [11], and the probabilistic model, among others.

In the sequel, we will introduce some retrieval performance measures that will be used in Chapter 5 of this book. For more information on information retrieval, we refer to [12-14].

Recall and precision are common measures used to characterize the retrieval performance of an information retrieval system. In order to define them let us introduce the following terms. Given the information request *I*, and a reference collection of documents, the system retrieves the answer set of documents *A*. Let *R* be the set of relevant document for the information request *I* provided by specialists (Figure 2.6 illustrates previously introduced sets). In that case, precision (*Pr*) and recall (*Rc*) are calculated as in equations 1 and 2 respectively.

$$\Pr = \frac{card(A \cap R)}{card(A)} \tag{1}$$

$$\mathrm{Rc} = \frac{card(A \cap R)}{card(R)} \tag{2}$$

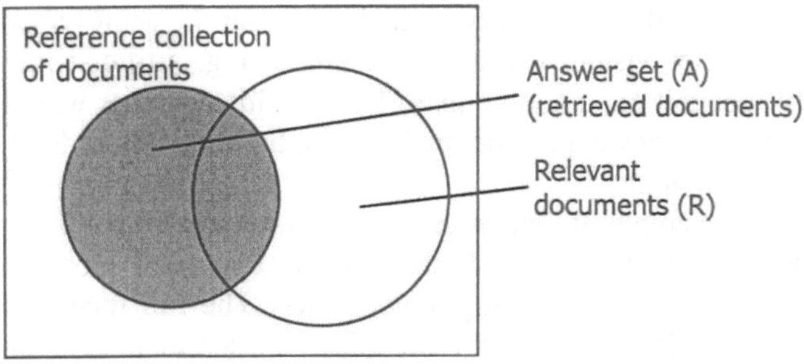

Figure 2.6. Document retrieval

The precision of the retrieval strategy is determined by measuring how many of the answers returned by the strategy are in fact correct. In contrast, the recall of the retrieval strategy determines how many of the documents that should have been retrieved by the strategy were in fact retrieved. The perfect information retrieval system would have recall and precision of both 1.

There are some more measures that characterize the retrieval performance of information retrieval systems, such as precision versus recall curve, effectiveness, and average search length, but as they are not used in this book, we refer to [15] for their description.

4. CONTENT-BASED VIDEO RETRIEVAL

Content-based image and video retrieval is a relatively new research topic. It has its roots in conventional information retrieval, aiming at the retrieval of information rather than the retrieval of data. Similarly to a text-based retrieval system, a content-based image or video retrieval system has to interpret the content of the documents of its collection (images or video records) and rank them according to the level of their relevance to the query. However, the obvious difference between text-based retrieval, image, and video retrieval is the nature of the documents in collection. Instead of words a content-based image or video retrieval system deals with collections of images or video records. Consequently, the system is confronted with the problem of image or video understanding. It has to gather key information about a document (an image or a video sequence) in order to better understand and interpret the content of that document. The information in these documents is highly unstructured and can take a visual form, but it can also come from other information sources, such as auditory or text-based. The content information has to be extracted from these multiple modalities through a process of interpretation, which relies on the achievements in the fields of computer vision, digital signal processing, artificial intelligence, and pattern recognition, among others. These fields, together with databases and information retrieval, provide fundamental building blocks for a content-based retrieval system.

To give an example of content-based video retrieval functionality, let us revisit our example movie database. Assume that each movie record is associated with the corresponding movie video. The full functionality of a content-based retrieval system would allow a user to pose a query like "select all videos that have car chasing and gunfire scenes".

4.1 Nature of video documents

In order to better understand why video retrieval must be so different from the traditional text information retrieval, let us consider the nature of video documents. The main difference between video documents and traditional alphanumeric documents is that the former use different modalities to convey information to users. Typical modalities in a video document are: visual, auditory, and textual modality. Early research in the video arena focused mainly on visual modality. However, video documents contain speech, music, and other sounds. Furthermore, they very often include text that describe or give additional information to audio-visual content in the form of closed-captions, superimposed text, or transcripts.

Next to the multimodal nature of video data, there is more dissimilarity between video and alphanumeric documents. Hampapur and Jain [16] defined six criteria to compare these two classes: resolution, production process, ambiguity of interpretation, interpretation effort, data volume, and similarity.

The resolution is defined as the detail that a class of documents provides. A textual description of a scene provides a very abstract description. An image is worth a thousands words, according to the well-known saying. A video document, which contains so many images, consequently provides a much higher level of details than an alphanumeric document.

The production process takes into account the base, which is used to generate the documents. For an alphanumeric document this is a finite set of symbols (alphabet), while video documents, containing three different modalities, are generated from a much larger set of symbols.

The ambiguity of interpretation measures the number of interpretation derivable from the documents. Here, the multimodal and unstructured nature of video documents is again a distinguishing factor. Video documents comprise textual modality and extend to visual and auditory modalities. Especially these two modalities can be perceived differently by different people resulting in numerous interpretations of the same video data. Therefore, the number of interpretations of a video document is typically larger than for a text document.

The interpretation effort actually corresponds to the computational effort required to interpret a given unit of information. However, it is far more difficult to interpret a video document than an alphanumeric one. Video understanding requires much more efforts, as it will be shown a few times throughout this book.

Data volume considers a space requirement for the two classes of documents. Despite the obvious fact that video documents require much more space for storage than textual documents, let us give some more details of voluminous nature of video data. Digitized audio-visual information consists of continuous streams of digital samples of audio and video signals. An audio sample is represented by an integer value that usually corresponds to the amplitude of the audio signal at a time instant. The sampling is done with a fixed rate (usually 11025, 22050, or 48000 times per second). A video sample, i.e. a frame, represents the values of red, green, and blue of all pixels of a frame. A frame in a PAL video holds 768 x 576 pixels with a sampling rate of 25 frames per second[2]. Storage volume depends on the number of bits used for encoding this information. Usually, this is translated to more than 20 MB of storage space per second, 1.2GB per minute, and 72GB for an hour long video. Although compressing techniques reduce these numbers for more than 10 times, video data is quite voluminous.

The last criterion used by Hampapur and Jain to distinguish video from alphanumeric documents considers similarity between two units of the same class of documents. In the case of structured alphanumeric data, it is relatively well defined, while it is very difficult to define similarity of two video documents (multimodalities, temporality, etc.).

[2] Technically, a PAL video consists of 50 frames with resolution 768 x 288 per second, where 25 frames are for the even scan lines which are interlaced with 25 frames for odd scan lines.

All these differences of video data compared to traditional alphanumeric data make video data difficult to manage and confront a video database management system with many challenges.

4.2 Fundamentals of content-based video retrieval

The research on content-based visual information retrieval started in the early 90's. First systems concentrated on image data and its retrieval based on its visual content, such as color, texture, and shape. Video data was very soon taken into consideration. Early video retrieval systems only extended image retrieval systems with functionality for the segmentation of video into shots and the extraction of key-fames from these shots. On the other hand, the analysis of video content, which fully consider temporality of video, has been a very active research area for a couple of years and it is likely to attract even more attention in years to come.

Nowadays, a content-based video retrieval system identifies different processes and subsystem. A typical architecture of such a system is depicted in Figure 2.7.

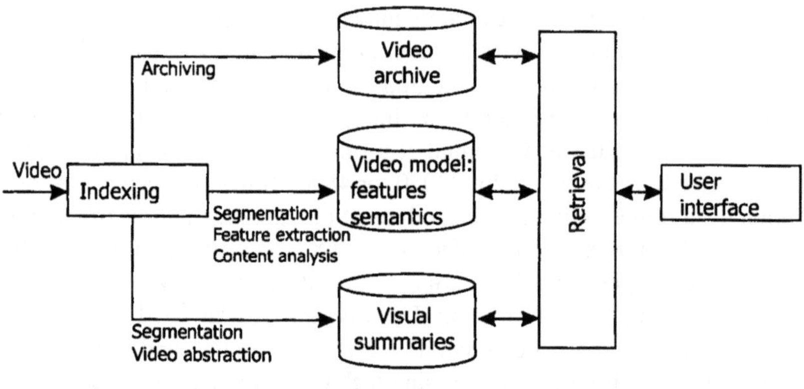

Figure 2.7. A generic block diagram of a content-based video retrieval system

The indexing phase deals with issues of inserting new video recordings into an existing collection. It is responsible for the creation of a video index, visual summaries, and a digital video archive. Usually, the indexing is done off-line.

With respect to the creation of a video index, which involves the extraction of the necessary information for instantiating a video data model, the indexing phase starts with the segmentation of video data into smaller pieces. This is done using video processing and pattern analysis tools. Next, the indexing phase includes the process of feature extraction and content analysis. The feature extraction, which is in most cases automatic, involves extraction of low-level features that characterize visual and audio content (for example color histogram). In this phase, a more sophisticated content analysis can be also performed. It includes the creation of a higher level representation of video content by extracting video objects and events. Nowadays, systems often offer this through a manual annotation of video content.

Video summaries are created in order to visualize and represent the units of video structure. They reduce the huge amount of information contained in video, supporting the process of video browsing and navigation. This is often done by extracting key-frames (images that represent the content of a shot in the best way) from video units and their organization into different structures, such as timeline, mosaic, or graph. Another possibility is to extract most representative video sequences that carry the highlights of video data, which is known as video skimming.

In the insertion process, a video may be digitized and compressed if needed. However, many videos come into the system directly in a digital compressed format. They are stored on a video server that manages the physical storage and ensures the streaming of video data.

The retrieval process deals with the extraction of video data from the database according to user queries. It involves transformation of a user query in a way that the query is mapped into a video data model representation, with the final goal of retrieving the desired information. This process is interconnected with the process of content analysis. For example, one can think of the retrieval process as the process of mapping a user query that specifies high-level video concepts to the low-level indices that represents low-level video content or even raw video data. On the other hand, in the case of a user query that specifies low-level features, the system often has to deal with finding similar feature vectors in a very high dimensional feature space [17].

The user interface is a very important component of a content-based retrieval system. It should make the process of query formulation easier, helping the user to articulate his information need. The user interface has to provide means for browsing and searching video data by example, sketch, low-level features, and semantic concepts. It has to be built bearing in mind that many users start retrieval process with the motto 'I know it when I see it'.

4.3 Searching video data

As video documents involve huge amounts of data from various media, the need to efficiently query this data becomes significant. Bearing in mind the nature of video data, we concentrate on specific issues of the query process in this subsection.

Video documents are often well structured in a similar way as books are organized into chapters and sections (the next chapter explains this in more details). Therefore, in most number of cases, the video structure can be queried using well-developed techniques of the existing technology. For example, the search process in video models that have a hierarchical structure (see Section 2.3 of Chapter 3) is usually based on free-text/attributes/keywords information in the nodes of the tree. What it has to take into account is a hierarchical organization of nodes. For instance, if a node's ancestor is in the query result set, the descendant node should be removed from the result set. Another problem could be caused by a stratification approach [18]. In this approach, textual descriptors, called strata, are associated with possibly overlapping portions of a linear video stream. This means that one video unit could be part of several different strata. If a query results in more than one stratum, duplication of video units should be avoided. Examples of composition operators that are defined to handle this problem can be found in [19, 20].

Video content can be queried at different levels. Traditional query languages provide facilities to query bibliographic video data. However, after watching a video, humans often forget names and other attributes related to video, but remember the content of a video in terms of visual content or objects and different events that appeared. Users also want to be able to find a particular part of a video that is the subject of their interests. Therefore, a video search engine should provide ability to directly retrieve information based on audio-visual content, which is more challenging. Content-based retrieval can be performed on the audio-visual features such as color histogram, textures, shapes, or on the semantic level that is much more complex.

4.3.1 Querying the features

Querying at the feature level is a common technique used in content-based image retrieval. The most classical aspect of this kind of search is query by example search. A user specifies an image as an example and searches for images that are most similar to it. The system ranks images in the database according to similarity algorithm and presents the high ranked images to the user. The similarity algorithm measures similarity between the features of the query image and the features of each image from the database. Possible types of similarity measurements could be based on a color distribution, texture, shape, and spatial information contained within the visual scenes. A screenshot from a prototype image retrieval system developed in the UCSB Alexandria Digital Library project, called NETRA [21] is presented in Figure 2.8. The system uses color, texture, shape, and spatial location information in segmented image regions to search and retrieve similar regions from the database.

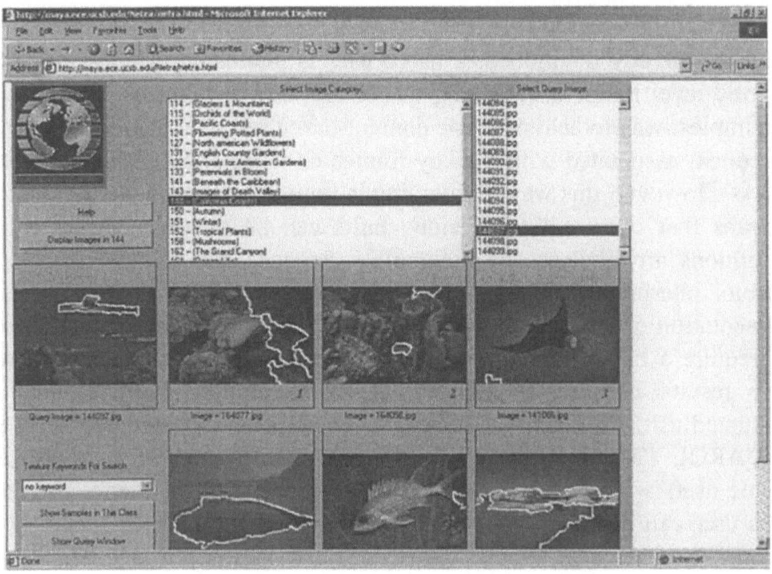

Figure 2.8. Query by example approach (NETRA system [21])

This technique can also be used in video retrieval systems. In the video field, querying on the feature level is usually based on key-frame similarity measurement. After the segmentation of a video into shots and the selection of representative frames (key-frames), the query problem on a video becomes similar to the one on a set of images.

Next, images and videos can be searched by a visual sketch. A user draws a visual sketch of an image or video clip he has in mind. By drawing, he specifies low-level features that are used in the similarity search process. These approaches are often media specific, i.e. they consider only one media type in isolation (in most cases visual modality).

Finally, querying the features can be done by a direct specification of features, which is sometimes used by users with a deeper technical background. Typical features involve color, texture, object's shape, and motion properties. Motion is a good candidate that could be considered as an attribute to be used in organizing and retrieving video data. It is attributed to a global (camera) motion and a local (object) motion. The MovEase video retrieval system [22] is an example of an approach that uses motion as a primary attribute in video retrieval. However, rather than simple motion primitives, a user would more likely choose to describe a scene in terms of high-level concepts.

4.3.2 Querying the semantics

As we already mentioned, a naive user is interested in querying at the semantic level rather than having to use features to describe his concepts. The simplest way to achieve basic content-based retrieval is to use keywords or free-text associated with the key-frames or video shots in the annotation process. However, this way of querying is limited by the annotation process. It means that only annotated video units can be queried. Moreover, the descriptions are likely to be incomplete, because one can not foresee all possible interpretations of the same content during indexing. Also, representation of one segment of video data by a large number of keywords will require a big storage space. Finally, users might not be satisfied with query results because of subjectivity of annotations. Queries may be formulated using the standard query language, or an extension of SQL, e.g. the CAROL [23] or VideoSQL [20] query language. Some approaches provide users with the ability to define the scope of their queries. It means that a user can decide if he wants to use annotations that are made by the system, by other users, or by himself. An example is the WVTDB system [24]. Symbols or icons may be used as a visual interface in the query process [25].

An extension of this basic principle is to provide facilities for querying additional video entities that are subjects of interests in video. It allows two types of information to be queried in the video database system: (1) entities that appear in video sequences and (2) video frames in which some of these entities are present. The second type is usually performed using the contain-predicate that checks whether or not an entity is in a particular video unit. An example of the SQL-like query language, called VIQS, that enables this type of querying, is developed by Hwang and Subrahmanian [26].

Query languages that use spatio-temporal operations are more powerful, because they provide sub-frame data access based on spatio-temporal characteristics. An underlying model of these query languages is able to manipulate video entities that are subject of users' interest. These entities are associated with sub-frames. In addition, the temporal aspect is also taken into account. Therefore, a user is able to specify very detailed complex queries as Boolean combinations of spatial operators including topological, directional, and distance operators, as well as temporal operators including point and interval operators. For example, a user can specify the query "Find a video clip in which a dog approaches Mary from the left", using the

Multimedia Object Query Language - MOQL [27], which is a general-purpose multimedia query language based on the Object Query Language (OQL). In a similar way, the query language based on the LHDVM model [28] supports queries such as "Find video clips in which a police car with siren on is chasing a red Porsche and crashes into it". Another example is VEVA [29], a formal visual language, which is rooted in the functional data models. It is used to represent objects, motion, relationships, and synchronization concepts, allowing a user to draw a trajectory and then retrieve objects with a similar kind of motion.

4.3.3 Mixed approaches

Many systems integrate querying at the feature level with querying at the semantic level. In most cases, querying by example or by sketching is combined with annotation-based querying. However, other kinds of information can also be included. For example, the Virage system [30] allows a user to specify combined queries based on key-frames, primitive motion extractions (scale 0-100), captions, and audio primitives. Ardizone et al. in [31] proposed querying using a combination of motion features and dominant color. On the other hand, VideoQ [32] allows a user to query by sketching the scene and associating objects with different attributes and simple spatio-temporal relations.

Other systems enable users to make queries by combining expressions, using different spatial and temporal operators. In addition to that, new kinds of extensions are introduced by different query languages. For example, MOQL [27] introduced the document expression that incorporates primitives for querying structured documents that conform to the SGML[3] standard. Therefore, MOQL can be used for both document content retrieval and media content retrieval. Another example is the content-based video query language (CVQL), developed by Kuo and Chen [33]. In addition to a set of operations for specifying temporal and spatial relationships in queries, this query language defines a set of modifiers to enhance the power of predicate specifications and a macro mechanism to simplify the query specification.

A system that facilitates search over video data should also have a possibility to deal with imprecise information and uncertain interpretations of multimedia objects. Besides exact searches, it should support inexact searches on video objects. A user should be able to assign different weights to search conditions. These weights express the importance of the search conditions, as well as a user's uncertainty on some parts of the query. The result of the query is usually a ranked list of objects and recognition degree

[3] SGML stands for Standard Generalized Markup Language

pairs. An example of such a query language is the Multimedia Symbolic Query Language (MMSQL) proposed by Amato et al. [34].

4.4 MPEG-7

MPEG-7, formally known as 'Multimedia Content Description Interface' is a standard that describes multimedia content. Defined by the Moving Picture Coding Experts Group (MPEG), it has the ability to describe the low-level features, high-level content representations, and structural aspects of audio-visual data. The MPEG-7 standard specifies a rich set of description structures for audio-visual content, which can be instantiated by an application that analyses video content and used by other applications that search audio-visual data. The goal of the standard is to enable interoperability among applications and devices that deal with audio-visual content, including both ones that analyze and others that search the content. As shown in Figure 2.9, the standard does not cover the processes of description generation and consumption. The extraction of features and semantic concepts from multimedia data, as well as specifications of search engines and other programs that use these descriptions are out of the scope of this standard. An overview of the standard is provided in [35].

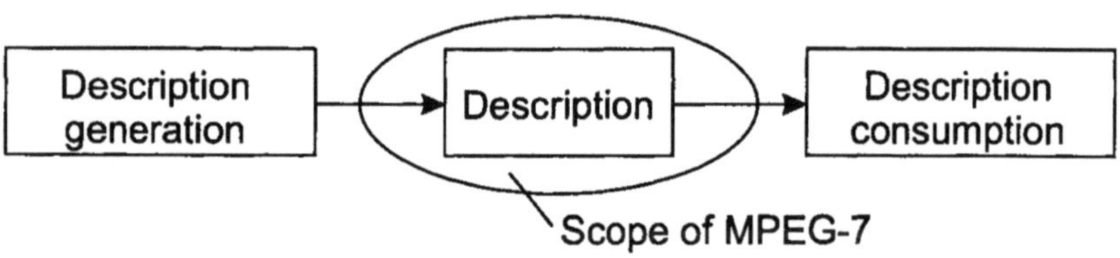

Figure 2.9. Scope of MPEG-7 standard

Practically, MPEG-7 standardizes:

1. a set of descriptors,
2. a set of description schemes,
3. description definition language, and
4. ways to encode descriptions.

A descriptor defines the syntax and semantics for the representation of an elementary feature. A feature can represent an audio-visual characteristic, such as color, texture, motion, etc, but also an attribute, such as the title or the author of the video.

A description schema specifies the structure and semantics of the relationships between its components that might be descriptors and description schemes. Description schemes are designed primarily to describe higher level audio-visual content, such as regions, objects, events, etc. They can be used to produce complex descriptions by integrating multiple descriptors and description schemes, as well as relations between them. The description schemes are grouped into three categories affecting visual, audio, and multimedia domains. The first two consider specific features unique to these two domains, while the latter includes description schemes that aim at content description by a combination of audio, visual, and textual data.

The description definition language (DDL) specifies description schemes. It can also be used by developers for the creation of new description schemes and descriptors, as well as for the extension and modification of existing description schemes, according to the specific needs of an application (see Figure 2.10). The DDL is an extension of the XML schema language [36]. It introduces new data types like histograms.

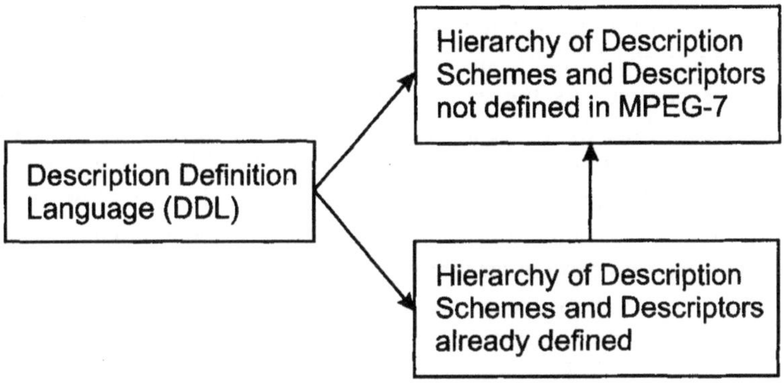

Figure 2.10. DDL, descriptors, and description schemes

Finally, the standard covers different representation (textual and binary), which are used to broadcast MPEG-7 data. A textual form of MPEG-7 descriptions is suitable for editing and searching, while the binary form is used for storage and streaming.

MPEG-7 aims at supporting a broad range of applications, such as digital libraries or home entertainment devices. It supports editing and reuse of audio-visual content, as well as searching multimedia content in large content archives. Even the audio-visual data on the web will be searchable provided that it is coupled with MPEG-7 descriptions.

5. SUMMARY

This chapter reviews fundamental principles of databases, considering in the first place data modeling and architecture issues. It presents an example of a database management system, which will be used later on in this book to provide the basis for the implementation of a prototype of a content-based video retrieval system. The presented database management system is based on the Monet database kernel with the Moa framework on the top of it. The advantages of this database platform, that have influenced our decision to chose it in our research, are its extensibility at all levels, as well as the main memory query execution and parallelism.

Next, the chapter moves focus to information retrieval and content-based video retrieval. The main goal of a video retrieval system is to support an efficient and easy way for users to retrieve the video data describing its content. It is very important for users to be capable of retrieving the video data specifying the content, since what they often remember and want to query is the content. As the video content can be approached at different levels (the raw data, feature, and concept level), querying at all these levels should be possible. In other words, a user should be able to query the video database combining the raw data, features, objects, and events. For instance, consider a user who wants to find some shots from the video that he watched a while ago. He may remember that in the specific shot, he was interested in, the dominant color was green. He may also remember some objects that appeared. Another user remembers the shape of an object and an action that took place in that shot. From the comprehensive survey given in this chapter, we can conclude that neither one of the reviewed systems and research proposals supports homogeneous querying at all levels of content representation. One goal of our research is to propose a system that will overcome the drawbacks of the existing approaches. As it was stated in Chapter 1, that system has to support the homogeneous querying and exploit multimodalities involved in video documents. In order to do so, the system must be able to deal with all different variations of video content representations, as well as to provide numerous mechanisms for mapping among distinct kinds of content. And this is exactly the subject of the next chapters.

RFERENCES

[1] Elmasri, S. B. Navathe, *Fundamentals of Database Systems*, Addison-Wesley, third edition, 2000.

[2] T. Tsichritzis, A. Klug, "The ANSI/X3/SPARC DBMS framework report of the study group on database management systems, *Information System*, No. 3, 1978, pp. 173-191.
[3] E.F. Codd, "A relational model of data for large shared data banks", *Communications of the ACM*, 13(6), 1970, pp. 377-387.
[4] C. J. Date, *An Introduction to Database Systems*, Addison-Wesley, third edition, 1985.
[5] R. Cattell, ed., *The Object Database Standard: ODMG, Release 2.0*, Morgan Kaufmann, 1997.
[6] E. Bertino, L. Martino, *Object Oriented Database Systems, Concepts and Architecture*, Addison-Wesley, 1993.
[7] P. Boncz, A.N. Wilschut, M.L. Kersten, "Flattering an object algebra to provide performance", *IEEE International Conference on Data Engineering*, Orlando, 1998, pp. 568-577.
[8] A.P. de Vries, *Content and Multimedia Database Management Systems*, PhD Thesis, Centre for Telematics and Information Technology, Enschede, the Netherlands, 1999.
[9] P. Boncz, M.L. Kersten, Monet: "An Impressionist Sketch of an Advanced Database System", *Basque International Workshop on Information Technology*, San Sebastian, 1995.
[10] A. N. Wilschut, R. van Zwol, J. Flokstra, "Road collapse in Magnum", In *Proceedings of the sixth International Symposium on Advances in Geographic Information Systems* (ACMGIS'98), 1998.
[11] G. Salton, C. Yang, A. Wong, "A vector-space model for automatic indexing", *Communications of ACM*, 18(11), 1975, pp. 613-620.
[12] R. Baeza-Yates, B. Ribeiro-Neto, *Modern Information Retrieval*, ACM Press, 1999.
[13] D. A. Grossman, O. Frieder, *Information Retrieval: Algorithms and Heuristics*, Kluwer International Series in Engineering and Computer Science, Kluwer Academic Publishers, 1998.
[14] C. J. van Rijsbergen, *Information Retrieval*, second edition, Butter-worths, 1979.
[15] A. del Bimbo, *Visual Information Retrieval*, Morgan Kaufmann, 1999.
[16] A. Hampapur, R. Jain, "Video Data Management Systems: Metada and Architecture" in *Multimedia Data Management*, A. Sheth, W. Klas (ed.), McGraw-Hill, 1998.
[17] C. Boehm, S. Berchtold, D.A. Keim, "Searching in high-dimensional spaces: Index structures for improving the performance of multimedia databases", *ACM Computing Surveys*, 33(3), 2001.
[18] T. G. Aguierre Smith, G. Davenport, "The Stratification System: A Design Environment for Random Access Video", *Proc. 3rd Inter. Workshop on Network and operating system Support for Digital Audio and Video*, La Jolla, CA, 1992.
[19] R. Weiss, A. Duda, D. K. Gifford, "Content-based Access to Algebraic Video", *Proc. of Int. Conf. on Multimedia Computing and Systems*, IEEE Press, 1994. pp. 140-151.
[20] E. Oomoto, K. Tanaka, "OVID: Design and Implementation of a Video-Object Database System", *IEEE Transaction on Knowledge and data Engineering*, Vol. 5, No. 4, Avgust, 1993, pp. 629-643.
[21] W. Y. Ma and B. S. Manjunath, "NETRA: A Toolbox for navigating large image databases", In *the Proceedings of the IEEE Intl. Conf. Image Processing* (ICIP'97), Santa Barbara, October 1997.
[22] G. Ahanger, D. Benson, T.D.C. Little, "Video Query Formulation", *Storage and retrieval for Images and Video Databases II*, San Jose, 1995.
[23] Q. Li, Y, Yang, W-K. Chung, "CAROL: Towards a Declarative Video Data Retrieval Language", *Proc. of SPIE*, Vol. 3561, 1998, pp. 69-78.

[24] H. Jiang, A. Elmagarmid, "WVTDB – a semantic content-based videotext database system on the world wide web", *IEEE Transactions Knowledge and Data Engineering*, 10 (6) 1998, pp. 947-966.

[25] M. Davis, "Knowledge Representation for Video", *Proc. of 12th National Conference on Artificial Intelligence*, Vol. 1, Seattle, Washington, 1994, pp. 120-127.

[26] E. Hwang, V.S. Subrahmanian, "Querying Video Libraries", *J. of Visual Communications and Image Representation*, Vol. 7, No. 1, March 1996.

[27] J. Z. Li, *Modeling and Querying Multimedia Data*, Technical Report TR 98-05, Laboratory for Database System Research, University of Alberta, Canada, March 1998.

[28] H. Jiang, A. Elmagarmid, "Spatial and temporal content-based access to hypervideo databases" *VLDB Journal*, 1998, No. 7, pp. 226-238.

[29] F. Golshani, N. Dimitrova, "A Language for Content-Based Video Retrieval", *Multimedia Tools and Applications*, 6 (3), 1998, pp. 289-312.

[30] A. Hampapur, A. Gupta, B. Horowitz, C-F. Shu, C. Fuller, J. Bach, M. Gorkani, R. Jain, "Virage Video Engine", *SPIE* Vol. 3022, 1997.

[31] E. Ardizzone, M. La Cascia, D. Molinelli, "Motion and Color Based Video Indexing and Retrieval", *Intl. Conf. on Pattern Recognition*, ICPR, Wien, Austria, Aug. 1996.

[32] S-F. Chang, W. Chen, H. Meng, H. Sundaram, D. Zhong, "A Fully Automated Content Based Video Search Engine Supporting Spatio-Temporal Queries", *IEEE Transaction on Circuits and Systems for Video Technology*, Vol. 8, No. 5, Sept., 1998.

[33] T. C.T. Kuo, A. L.P. Chen, "A Content-Based Query Language for Video Databases", *Proc. of IEEE Multimedia Computing Systems*, 1996.

[34] G. Amato, G. Mainetto, P. Savino, "An Approach to a Content-Based Retrieval of Multimedia Data" *Multimedia Tools and applications*, Vol. 7, No. 1/2, 1998, pp. 5-36.

[35] J.M. Martinez, *MPEG-7 Overview*, ISO/IEC JTC1/SC29/WG11, Klangenfurt, July 2002, http://mpeg.telecomitalialab.com/standards/mpeg-7/mpeg-7.htm

[36] D. C. Fallside (Ed.), *XML Schema part 0: Primer*, May 2001. http://www.w3.org/TR/xmlschema-0/

Chapter 3

VIDEO MODELING

1. INTRODUCTION

Content-based video retrieval requires changes in a multimedia database management system relative to a traditional database management system. These changes take effect mainly with respect to modeling and querying techniques. As stated in [1], a multimedia data model should be different from a traditional data model. First of all, a video data model has to manage all modalities involved in a video document, i.e. visual, auditory, and textual modalities. Next, a multimedia data model should include the elements that represent the content of these modalities, together with the elements that represent their inherent structural properties. It should be able to capture and represent various types of information about multimedia objects, their structures, operations, and properties, as well as real-world objects and relationships among them. Therefore, it has to provide a sophisticated representation of video content in terms of low-level features and high-level concepts, and enable satisfactory retrieval capabilities. In a multimedia environment, browsing has additional importance and queries can be based not only on an exact matching but also on degrees of similarity, which has to be supported starting from the data model.

As far as video modeling is concerned, we can make distinction between two important items that should be modeled: the structure and the content of a video. Structural elements of a video are derived by the portioning of a video into small manageable units. The modalities involved in a video document have a temporal dimension, which is one of the most important factors that a good model of video structure should be able to express. In addition to the structure, the content of a video should be modeled. The semantics, as interpretation of the information that video conveys, allows a user to retrieve the video data based on content. A video data model has to provide a solid base for the system that will support an automatic process of inferring semantics from raw video data.

This chapter deals with the mentioned video modeling issues with emphasis on the last one, i.e. the support for content-based retrieval. The next two sections address modeling of the video structure and content, respectively. Section 4 discusses video models presented in the previous two sections and brings some conclusions. In order to overcome the drawbacks of data models surveyed, a video modeling framework, called Cobra, is introduced in Section 5. Finally, Section 6 describes the set-up for the Tennis case study, which will be a leading example through the next chapters. Section 7 summarizes the chapter.

2. COARSE-GRAINED STRUCTURING

Video, as a media, conveys large amounts of information that require large volumes of raw data. If we want to provide tools for managing and querying these large data volumes, the primary requirement is the construction of the video structure. The fundamental video units should be identified, as well as the segmentation criteria that will be used in detecting boundaries between consecutive video elements. The video elements have to be organized in a structure that supports storing, editing, and retrieval of video data in an efficient manner.

2.1 Segmentation

A video document consists of different modalities, i.e. information channels, which are used to express the author's ideas. Although visual and auditory channels are most commonly used, textual modality is also very often present, for example, in the form of closed-captions. As each of these modalities has a different elementary unit, which is sampled with a different frequency, it will be very difficult to segment a video based on a unified criteria. Therefore, the most approaches use mainly visual modality while segmenting a video into smallest units.

The elementary physical unit of the visual video structure is an image frame. However, it is rarely the unit of users' interest because there are so many frames even in a very short video (25 frames in a second, 1500 in a minute, and 90K in an hour of a PAL video). Shots, i.e. sequences of frames generated during a continuous camera operation, are obviously fundamental units of the video structure. So, the first step in the building of a video structure is to segment a video document into shots, i.e. to detect transitions from one shot to another.

There are two types of shot transitions: abrupt and gradual. The abrupt change between last frame of a shot and the first frame of a subsequent shot is the simplest transition, called cut. The gradual transitions include: fades, dissolve, wipes, etc. There are two types of fades: fade-in and fade-out. A fade-in means to gradually start a shot from a black screen, while a fade-out is often used as a transitional device from full intensity image to black. A dissolve is a transition from one shot to the next where the first gradually fades-out as the second gradually fades-in with some overlap between the two. A wipe is a moving transition of a frame across the screen that enables one shot to gradually replace another.

There are a number of different algorithms developed for the detection of cuts in video documents. Marques and Furht [2] classified them into seven groups: pixel-based, statistics-based, histogram-based, transform-based, edge-based, motion-based, and other. The gradual transitions are more difficult to detect. There are three main groups of approaches. The first uses every k-th frame, the second is the statistical one based on effect modeling, while the third models the effect of a transition on intensity edges in subsequent frames. For an extensive overview of a number of different algorithms developed for the detection of shot boundaries we refer to [2-5].

2.2 Time-line models

All video modalities have a temporal component. Therefore the video structure should be able to express temporality. As video elements span different amounts of time, a video retrieval system must provide facilities that will take care of the position of a specific element in the whole document, its duration, start, and end frame, as well as of temporal relations between video elements. Consequently, temporal modeling in the context of video management systems has recently attracted substantial attention.

Early video modeling approaches [6] used a timeline that gives explicit, static, temporal relations between video elements on time axis. These traditional approaches organize video units (units of all modalities involved in video) in chronological sequences (an example is given in Figure 3.1). The inter- and intra-modality synchronizations are defined by the explicit binding to the time-line.

The time-line model is inherited from storyboards, which are used in film production. It gives a rather direct representation of a video document and as such it is exploited in many video editing tools. Each individual shot has explicit timing, which eases the playing of the whole video document, but at the same time complicates the editing process. In the case of editing, extra efforts are needed for maintaining inter-modality synchronization. Furthermore, the time-line model does not support structures, i.e. higher-level abstractions of basic video elements, which allow user to group video elements into semantically meaningful units. Hierarchical models overcome this limitation.

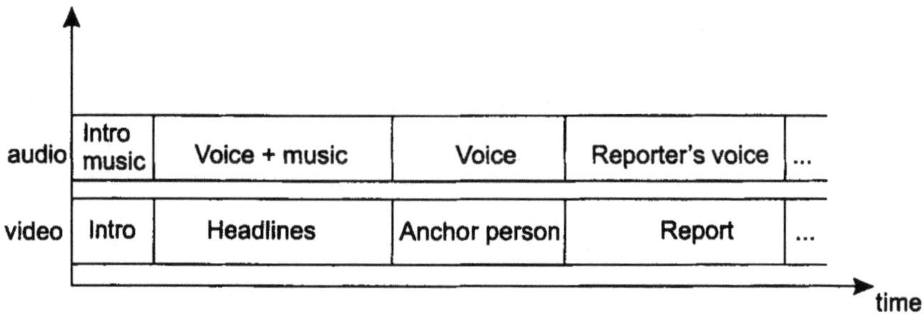

Figure 3.1. Time-line example for a news video

2.3 Hierarchical models

As video is a structured medium, in which objects and events convey stories in time and space, it has to be considered as a document and not as an unstructured sequence of frames or shots. Many researchers agree with a hierarchical structure of a video that enables creation of complex video units by combining elementary units or recursively by combining complex units. The most often proposed hierarchies have a story-scene-shot-frame structure (Figure 3.2). The terms frame and shot are defined in Section 2.1. A scene is a collection of usually adjacent shots, focusing on the same objects or describing the same actions that are related in time and space. A story is a group of scenes that linked together give a meaning. This type of hierarchy is discussed in [7] in more details.

A simple way to compose a hierarchy of video units is to introduce nesting. It means that fundamental video elements (portions of a linear video stream) can be organized hierarchically as nodes in a tree. As a benefit, nested relationships between the nodes allow user to explore the context in which a node appears. Examples of such an approach are the algebraic video data model [8] and the video-object database system - OVID [9].

Hierarchical video models deal with two different video segmentation criteria: syntactic and semantic [10]. As already described, syntactic criteria segment video into sequences of frames (shots) generated during a continuous camera operation. On the other hand, higher-level segmentation, i.e. grouping shots into scenes or scenes into story units, generally requires semantic criteria and a higher level of content analysis. It is a much more challenging task than shot detection, because scenes and stories are entities that are inherently subjective and lack universal definition and rigid structure with respect to raw video data. The strategies used for automatic scene detection are based on explicit models of video documents [11, 12] or rules related to film theory, a scene transition graph, or statistical techniques. The integrated use of different video modalities, which is pioneered by Informedia project [13], is an emerging trend in this research area. For a brief description of various methods and pointers to the literature we refer to [14].

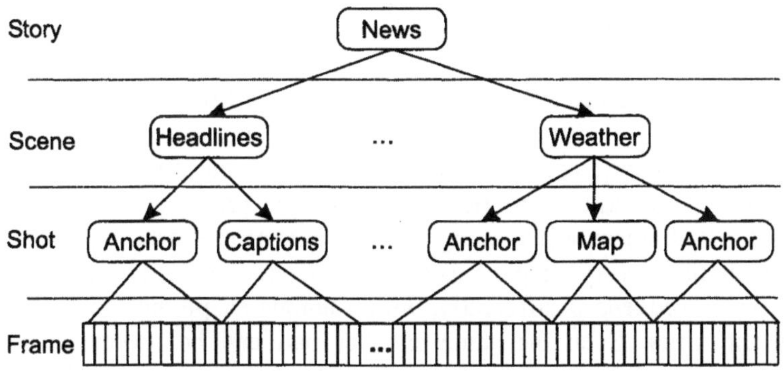

Figure 3.2. Common structure imposed on a news video

A hierarchical structure is also used by approaches that extract objects and/or events that appear in a video. They segment a video and compose a hierarchical video structure according to occurrence of common objects and/or events in a video. They usually associate an object/event or a group of objects/events with a set of frame sequences. These approaches model the structure of a video considering the video content in the first place. An example is the Common Video Object Tree (CVOT) model [15], where a tree structure is used to represent groups of video units. The next section will bring a more detailed description of these approaches.

The hierarchical models support a structured top-down approach and relative timing of video units (nodes), which eases editing and reuse of composite objects. However, manipulation and presentation of video units within a hierarchical video structure is impossible without appropriate video operations. For example, if a user, browsing the video structure, decides to see a video sequence associated with a specific inner node of the hierarchy, a video retrieval system should generate a composition of the video sequences associated with all children of this node. To make this possible, first, we need an operation that creates the most primitive video expression, e.g. a presentation of a video segment. Then, we need operations that create compound expressions. They specify composition, i.e. define temporal relationships between primitive video expressions. Examples of such operations are concatenation, union, intersection, etc. Very rich sets of video operations are proposed in an algebraic data model [8] and the work of Adiba et al. [16].

3. FINE-GRAINED INTERPRETATION

In the literature, video content is approached at different levels: raw data, low-level visual content (features), and semantic content (concepts). The raw video data consists of elementary video units together with some general video attributes, such as format, frame rate, etc. The low-level visual content is characterized by visual features, such as color, shapes, textures, and motion. The semantic content contains high-level concepts, such as objects and events. The same semantic concept can be presented through many different visual presentations using different sets of raw data. Let us look at an example of the very simple concept of a snooker ball. It can be presented in two video sequences differently, with a unique shape, but with different colors and sizes. Even the same snooker ball can be presented with a different size in different sets of raw data, due to zoom effects. If we talk about more complex concept, such as a car, or some concepts that include temporality, we can end up with a very long list of possible low-level representations of the same concept. Furthermore, the same visual data are perceived and interpreted differently by different people. Therefore, there is no evident direct mapping between high-level concepts and raw video data.

It is obvious that requirements for the extraction of different types of video content are diverse. The process of extracting the semantic content is most complex, because it requires domain knowledge or user interaction, while extraction of visual features can be often done automatically and it is commonly domain independent.

3.1 Feature-based modeling

Extensive research efforts have been made with regard to the retrieval of video and image data based on their audio-visual content such as color distribution, texture, and shape [2, 17-20]. As already mentioned in Chapter 2, most systems only support the retrieval of still images. Approaches that concentrate on the visual media alone fall into two categories: query by example and visual sketches. Both of these are based on similarity measurement. Possible types of similarity are color, texture, shape, and spatial similarity. Examples include VisualSEEk [21], Photobook [22], Surfimage [23], Blobworld [24], MUSE [2] as well as IBM's Query by Image Content (QBIC) [25], VideoQ [26], Virage video engine [27], Jacob [28], and CueVideo [29] in the field of video retrieval. The image retrieval systems allow a user to make queries based on visual content of an image, i.e. properties such as color percentages, color layout, and textures. Some of these systems use the spatial information and allow a user to make queries by sketching the layout of color regions (an example is presented in Figure 3.3), or by providing the URL of a seed image.

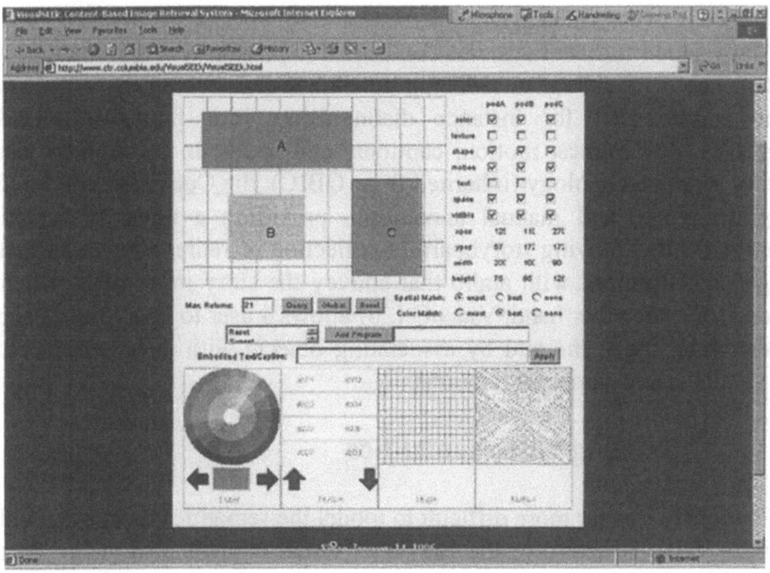

Figure 3.3. VisualSEEK system

Query by example approaches are suitable if a user has a similar image at hand, but they would not perform well if the image was taken from a different angle or had a different scale. The naive user is interested in querying at the semantic level rather than having to use features to describe his concepts. Sometimes, it is difficult to express concepts by sketching. Even then, good match in terms of the feature metrics may yield poor results in the context of concepts (multiple domain recall, e.g. a query for 60% of green and 40% of blue may return an image of grass and sky, a green board on a blue wall or a blue car parked in front of a park, as well as many others).

Early approaches in video retrieval borrowed techniques from image retrieval. They only added the functionality for key frame extraction to existing image retrieval systems. After key-frame extraction, they applied similarity measurements on them based on low-level features. This is not satisfactory because video is temporal media, so sequencing of individual frames creates new semantics that may not be present in any of the individual frames. Although there are many techniques for choosing key-frames, this is still a challenging problem. For example, Wolf in [30] used motion analysis, while in the Virage video engine [27], key-frames are obtained by analyzing first 30 seconds of each shot according to many parameters, such as: amount of motion, presence of skin-colored pixels, difference between frames, etc.

Many video retrieval systems combine this principle with a higher level content-based modeling, introducing new advanced techniques. The Virage video engine [27] for instance distinguishes four fundamental video primitives: key frames, motion, captions, and audio. In addition to visual content search technology (inherited from QBIC), the CueVideo system [29] integrates voice and manual annotation, providing a novel presentation technique called moving storyboard (a collection of representative animated images synchronized with audio that convey the story in a highly efficient manner). On the other hand, VideoQ [26] allows a user to query the database by sketching the scene and by associating objects with different attributes and simple spatio-temporal relations.

3.2 Modeling video semantics

Obviously it is far more difficult to model the semantic content of a video than the video structure or the low-level visual content of a video. At the physical level, video is a temporal sequence of pixel regions without a direct relation to its semantic content. Therefore, it is very difficult to explore semantic content from the raw video data. In addition, if we consider multiple semantic meaning such as metaphorical, associative, hidden, or suppressed meaning that the same video content may have, we make the problem even more complex.

The simplest way to model the video content is by using free text manual annotation. Early computerized video logging systems, such as one described in [5], divided a video into fixed segments (shots) and described every segment independently using free text and attribute/keywords annotation – as the semantic content description of a video segment. These approaches have been strongly criticized because of their inflexibility and many limitations. Fixed video segmentation enforces the only one segmentation of the original data. A segmented part of a video is separated from its context. Hence, the important contextual information about a video sequence is lost.

On the other hand, approaches that are more flexible use semantic criteria to segment a video into logical units based on extracted content. Practically, a video is expressed with a set of descriptions that have frame addresses. An example is the 'stratification' approach [31], which proposes segmenting the contextual information rather than segmenting contiguous frames. Textual descriptors, called strata, are associated with portions of a linear video stream. The method allows overlapping of descriptors by layering one on the top of the other (Figure 3.4). In this way, the meaning of each frame of a video can be derived from the union of all strata that overlap the frame. The method reduces descriptive overhead, allowing a user to build descriptions upon each other, rather than uniquely describe each frame separately.

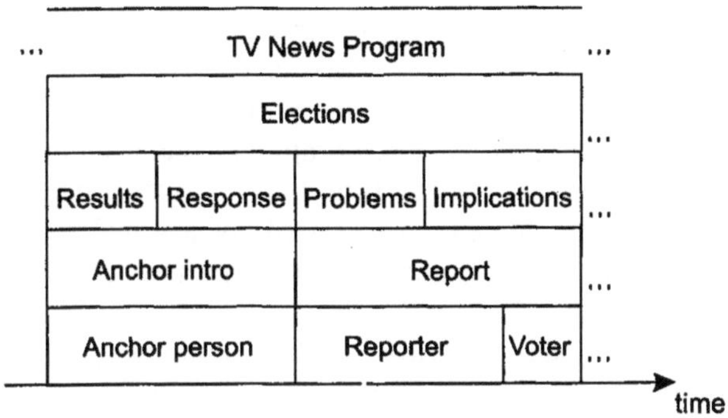

Figure 3.4. Modeling of a news video by the stratification approach

Some other approaches introduce additional video entities that should be annotated because they are subjects of interests in video. Besides these new video entities, their relationships should also be the first class citizens of the data model. For example, Adali et al. [32] define objects, events, and activities (event types) in their formal model of video data, called AVIS. Roles and players are also elements of this video model, because these two describe certain aspect of an activity. An interesting extension of this approach that allows the description of the contents of video sequences by capturing relationships between video entities and their attributes is done by Decleir et al. [33]. In addition to a formal definition of the video model, they propose a declarative, rule-based, constraint query language for video content-based indexing and retrieval. A knowledge-based approach for video modeling and querying, which also deals with video objects, is developed by Ardizzone and Hacid in [34]. They propose two abstract languages based on description logic: one for describing the video content and one for querying.

Limitations caused by a fixed vocabulary of keywords or predefined attributes could be overcome by using a schema-less approach. Such an approach supports the description of an arbitrary meaningful video frame sequence in a dynamic and incremental way. It is up to a user to define attributes of a video unit and their values. An example is the OVID system [9]. Another technique, which is introduced by this system, is interval inclusion inheritance. This mechanism, by which some attribute/value pairs of a video unit can be inherited by another video unit, enables sharing information among video units similarly to the stratification approach.

An important technique, which can also be used to speed up the process of annotation, as well as to make this process more user-friendly, is visualization. As far as annotation-based approaches are concerned, two items can be visualized. The first one is space of descriptors that are used for annotation of video units. Instead of the words, a user can use icons that are more descriptive. Icons, denoting objects and actions, can be grouped into a hierarchy of descriptive categories. They can also be combined to form compound descriptions. The second item that can be visualized is the process of annotation itself. A user can drag the icons from the hierarchy of descriptors space and drop them on time line to create temporally indexed annotations of the video content. An example of a visual language, which enables users to create multilayered, iconic annotations of video content, is Media Streams [35].

Another way to model the video entities assumes the use of spatio-temporal relations. The concept of video object can be associated to a sub-frame region that conveys useful information, while spatio-temporal relations among these objects can be defined as events. Video objects are characterized by their semantic and spatial properties, as well as relations to other video objects. Semantic information, such as the type of object, its name and other content information, can be associated with the object as free text, or if a domain knowledge is present as an OO model of the domain. The semantic associations among video object themselves, as well as with other logical video abstractions (e.g. events) can be done using hyperlinks, as in the Logical HyperVideo Data Model (LHVDM) [36].

Modeling of high-level concepts (objects and events) gives the possibility to describe objects in space and time and capture movements of objects. For example, Dimitrova and Golshani [37] model video by (object, motion, video) tuples in order to represent and retrieve video sequences by either one of the three representations.

As humans think in terms of events and remember different events and objects after watching a video, these high-level concepts are the most important cues in content-based retrieval. Let us take a soccer game as an example. Humans usually remember goals, interesting actions, red cards, etc.

Attempts to include these high-level concepts into video models have been made in [15, 36, 38].

There can be thousands of video objects and events in a single video, but only a small sub-set is useful and makes sense from users' point of view. Hence, only objects that are the subjects of interest should be considered. Another restriction that will reduce the number of objects is to consider objects only in the period of time when they are subjects of interest (not in the whole video). That is why, we can find in the literature the terms like "hot video object" [36] or "salient video object" [15].

Table 3.1. Modeling characteristics: 1-Audio, 2-Free-Text/Keywords, 3-Keyframes, 4-Features, 5-Objects, 6-Events, 7-Domain Modeling, 8-Temporality, 9-Motion, 10-Spatial Relations; (√: yes, -√: partially, -: no, ?: no information)

System\function	1	2	3	4	5	6	7	8	9	10
Virage	√	√	√	√	-	-	-	-	-√	-
VideoQ	-	√	√	√	√	-	-	-√	√	-√
QBIC	-	√	√	√	√	-	-	-	√	√
Jacob	-	-	√	√	-	-	-	-	-	-
Amato et al.	√	-	-	√	√	-	√	√	-	√
Informedia	√	√	√	-√	√	-	-	√	-√	√
VEVA	-	?	-	√	√	√	√	-√	√	-√
OVID	-	√	-	-	-	-	√	-	-	-
Algebraic Video	-√	√	-	-	-	-	-	-√	-	-
AVIS	-	-√	-	-	√	√	-√	-√	-	-
Decleir et al.	-	-√	-	-	√	-	√	-√	-	-
CVOT	-	√	-	-	√	√	√	√	-√	√
LHVDM	-	√	-	-	√	√	-	√	-√	√
Media Streams	-√	√	-	-	√	√	?	√	-√	-√

4. DISCUSSION

Table 3.1 summarizes the important characteristics of major contributions to the field with regard to video modeling. Performance measures of the systems based on described models are not included, since, to the best of our knowledge, the systems have never been tested on the same data sets. The distinction, we made with regard to the modeling of video content, which can be also seen from the Table 3.1, makes clear two important things. On the one hand, feature-based models (the upper half of Table 3.1) use automatically extracted features to represent the video content, but they do not provide semantics that describe high-level concepts of a video, such as objects and events. On the other hand, semantic models (bottom half of Table 3.1) usually use free text/attribute/keywords annotation to represent the high-level concepts of the video content that results in many drawbacks. The main one is that a search process is based only on the predefined attribute information, which is associated with video segments manually by human in the process of annotation. Furthermore, manual annotation is tedious, subjective, and time consuming. Obviously, an integrated approach, that will provide automatic mapping from raw video data to features and subsequently to high-level concepts, is a challenging solution.

A few domain dependent approaches, e.g. in soccer, American football, and tennis domain [39-41], show that detection of the ball, players, and even the part of the court is feasible. These approaches demonstrate that automatically extracted objects can be used in the process of content-based retrieval. Hence, more attention should be paid to the modeling of interactions and relations among these entities.

As we already mentioned, automatic detection of video objects (sub-frame entities) in the known domain is feasible. A video object can be defined as a collection of video regions, which have been grouped together under some criteria defined by the domain knowledge. A region, as a contiguous set of pixels that is homogeneous in the features such as texture, color, shape, or motion, could be automatically extracted and tracked. Therefore, shape, color, texture, as well as primitive motion and object duration are the attributes that could be assigned to each object. Then, video objects may be grouped into higher semantic classes using a tree structure and the domain knowledge. Similar ideas are proposed by Chang et al. [26] and Golshani and Dimitrova [42]. However, a fully automatic mapping from features to semantic concepts for unconstrained domains is still extremely difficult and it is likely that this will not be achieved in the near future.

Audio, as one of the essential components of video, can also help in the process of extracting semantics from low-level features. Combined audio and visual video components can provide much more information than any of these media alone. Therefore, an integrated model will provide the usage of additional information that can be critical to the perception and understanding of video content. The Informedia project [13] has contributed in that sense. It has shown that a successful system for digital library creation and exploration should integrate different sources of information, such as video, audio, close caption text, and others if present.

5. COBRA VIDEO MODELING FRAMEWORK

Bearing in mind the drawbacks of the video models surveyed in the previous sections, we propose a video modeling framework, called Cobra (COntent-Based RetrievAl), which integrates the low level and high level video representations [43]. It guides the process of translating raw video data into features and high-level concepts, capturing video semantics. In this process, it supports the use of different video modalities. In contrast to the approaches mentioned in the prior sections, our modeling framework divides concepts between objects and events, as different ontological kinds. The layered structure of the framework is shown in Figure 3.5. It consists of four layers: the raw data, feature, object, and event layer.

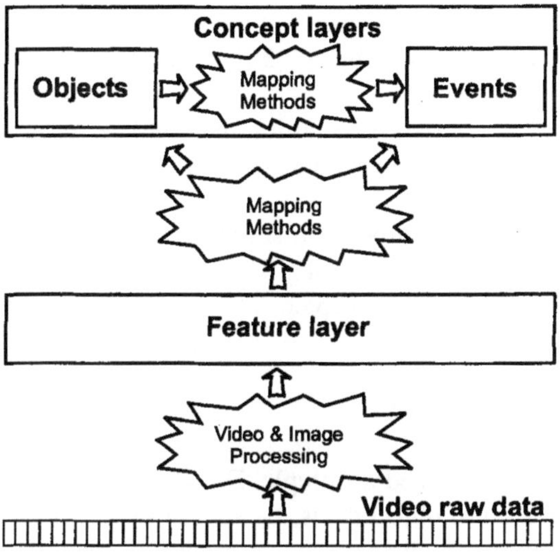

Figure 3.5. The layered hierarchy of the Cobra video modeling framework

The *raw video data layer* is at the bottom. This layer consists of a sequence of frames, as well as some video attributes, such as compression format, frame rate, number of bits per pixel, duration, etc. It also manages the hierarchical structure of video data.

The next layer is the *feature layer*, consisting of features that can be automatically extracted from raw data, characterizing colors, textures, shapes, and motion. They include some global features that characterize scenes, shots, or frames, and local features that characterize regions inside frames. Different video and image processing techniques can be used for their extraction.

The *concept layers* are on the top. They consist of logical concepts that are subject of interest to users or applications. Automatic mapping from the raw video data layer to the feature layer has been already achieved to a certain extent, but automatic mapping from the feature to the concept layers is still a challenging problem. We divide the concept layer into two ontologically different layers: the object and the event layer.

The *object layer* consists of entities (logical concepts), characterized by a prominent spatial dimension and assigned to regions across frames. A region is a contiguous set of pixels that is homogeneous in texture, color, shape, or motion properties. We consider a video object as a collection of regions that have been grouped together by some criteria defined by the domain knowledge. An object should also satisfy some conditions in a way that it is semantically consistent, representing one real-world object, and the subject of interest to some users or applications. Some examples of video objects are the player or the ball in a tennis game or the specific car in a car-race video. The terms, such as "hot video object" [36] or "salient video object" [15] are used for the same concept.

The *event layer* consists of entities that have a prominent temporal extent, describing the movements and interactions of different objects in a spatio-temporal manner.

In the sequel, we will introduce a simple notation, which is intended to help to better understand our modeling framework and the examples given at the end of this and the next chapter. The overall structure of our video framework is as follows:

$$V = (\Sigma, A, VS, F, O, E, AS)$$

The signature Σ is defined as a tuple, $\Sigma = (\Sigma_F, \Sigma_O, \Sigma_E, \Sigma_S)$. Σ_F is a set of feature types, Σ_O a set of object types, Σ_E a set of event types, and Σ_S is a set of audio segment types (audio clusters). A is a set of video attributes, such as frame sample rate, audio sample rate, file format, name, creation date, etc.

Video structure (VS) contains raw video data, which can be organized in a hierarchy of frames, shots, and scenes. Furthermore, it also contains frame regions (R). Each frame can comprise zero or more regions. Shots can comprise one or more frames and scenes one or more shots.

F is a set of video features. Each feature is described by its type descriptor ($\in \Sigma_F$), its value, and a reference to a frame or a region in a frame. Possible types of features include but are not limited to the ones defined in [44, 45].

O is a set of objects. An object is described by its type ($\in \Sigma_O$), identification, a set of regions that compose it, their features, as well as by the history of its geometry (minimum bounding rectangle) across frames. Video objects can be related to particular real-world objects that are modeled in the database (more details about this will be given in Chapter 6).

E is a set of events. An event is defined by its type ($\in \Sigma_E$), identification, a set of objects involved, and by the time interval it spans. Hence, event types are parameterized by using different object instances.

Audio structure (AS) is the counterpart of VS, containing audio data. The audio signal, as one of essential video components, provides a very rich source of information to supplement understanding of a video. Combining audio with other video information sources gives much more information than any information source alone. Therefore, we integrated audio primitives in the framework to provide additional information that might be crucial to the perception and understanding of video content. The raw audio data can be divided into speech and non-speech parts through the process of segmentation and classification (an example will be given in Chapter 5). A time-aligned transcript of the spoken words can be created using speech recognition, while semantic segmentation based on text can be used for obtaining the meaningful speech segments. The non-speech segments can be clustered and associated with textual descriptions.

6. TENNIS CASE STUDY

This section explains the instantiation of our modeling framework and necessary video preprocessing steps, using the Tennis case study as an example. The case study is intended to illustrate possible ways of the automatic extraction of semantic content from raw video data, serving as a leading example in this book. The aim of the case study is to automatically extract events like net-playing, rally, longest point, shortest point, and different kinds of tennis strokes from tennis videos. However, first of all, some preprocessing, which precedes the extraction of high-level concepts has to be done. It includes reconstruction of the video structure, i.e. the detection of shot boundaries, but also shot classification in our case study.

6.1 Video segmentation and shot classification

A typical video of a tennis match consists of different shots. The majority of shots show a tennis court with two players playing (playing shots in the sequel). However, there are also some advertisement and close up shots, as well as shots showing audience, which are usually taken during game breaks. Selection of the playing shots containing the tennis court from others is necessary in this case study, since our analysis focuses on the playing events. Therefore, the first step in our analysis would be to segment a tennis video into different shots. For this task, we use differences in color histograms of neighboring frames. A traditional histogram based algorithm [46] is modified in the sense that the histogram difference among several consecutive frames is calculated in order to gain robustness when dealing with digital effects like fades, dissolve, etc.

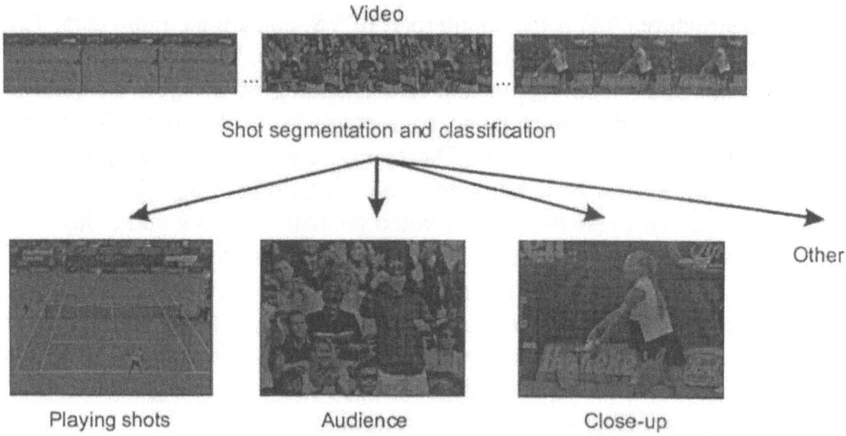

Figure 3.6. Shot detection and classification

For each frame in the video, we extract some global image features in order to be able to do segmentation and shot classification. The extracted features are: color histogram, dominant color, and entropy characteristics: mean and variance. The number of skin colored pixels is also calculated, but for each tenth frame in the shot.

The shot classification algorithm classifies shots based on some heuristics in four different categories: tennis, close-up, audience, and other (Figure 3.6). The court shots are recognized based on the dominant color. By analyzing the dominant color of all shots, the segmentation algorithm can be generalized to be able to work with different classes of tennis courts (clay, grass, and the different colors of the hard courts). The dominant color of the tennis court can be selected based on the percentage of pixels it covers in a frame, as well as on the number of frames it repeats in the video. A shot is classified as close-up, if it contains a significant amount of skin colored pixels. However, the audience shots can also contain a significant amount of skin colored pixels. The mean and variance of the image entropy characteristics are used in this case as distinguishing features. For a detailed description of extracted features, as well as of processes for their extraction we refer to [47].

6.2 Instantiation of the Cobra framework

In this subsection, we start with our modeling example. Here, we only initialize our video modeling framework, using the Tennis case study. This set-up serves as the basis for spatio-temporal formalization examples described in the next chapter.

First, the metadata for the tennis domain is described. Some video attributes are defined in set A, such as file format, frame rate, etc. The feature set consists of features that are described in the previous section: color histogram (f_1), dominant color (f_2), entropy characteristics mean (f_3) and variance (f_4), and the number of skin-colored pixels (f_5).

$\Sigma_F = \{f_1, f_2, f_3, f_4, f_5\}$,

The object, event, and audio segment types consist of the following elements:

Σ_O = {ball, net}
Σ_S = {cheering, stroke_sound, sigh_sound}
Σ_E = {service, volley, ace, player_near_the_base-line}

In the video parsing process presented in the previous subsection, we identified only basic video units, i.e. shots. Therefore, our VS set has elements of three types: *i*, *i*.F*j*, and *i*.F*j*.R*k*, where integer *i* points to the specific video shot, *i*.F*j*, to the frame *j* within the shot *i*, and *i*.F*j*.R*k* to the region *k* inside the frame *j*. Having a shot with three frames and the automatically extracted regions presented in Figure 3.7, the VS set will look like as follows:

VS = $\{s_1, s_1.f_1, s_1.f_1.r_1, s_1.f_1.r_2, s_1.f_1.r_3, s_1.f_1.r_4, s_1.f_1.r_5, \ldots, s_1.f_3, s_1.f_3.r_1, s_1.f_3.r_2, s_1.f_3.r_3, s_1.f_3.r_4\}$

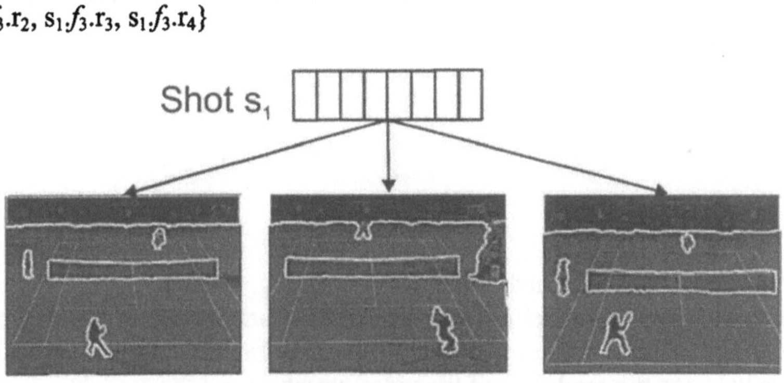

Figure 3.7. Shot, frames, regions

The values of features that are extracted in our preprocessing step are in the set F. As an example, Figure 3.8 visualizes extracted color histograms from two different frames. Note the difference in the color histograms of the two frames, which is used for the shot boundary detection.

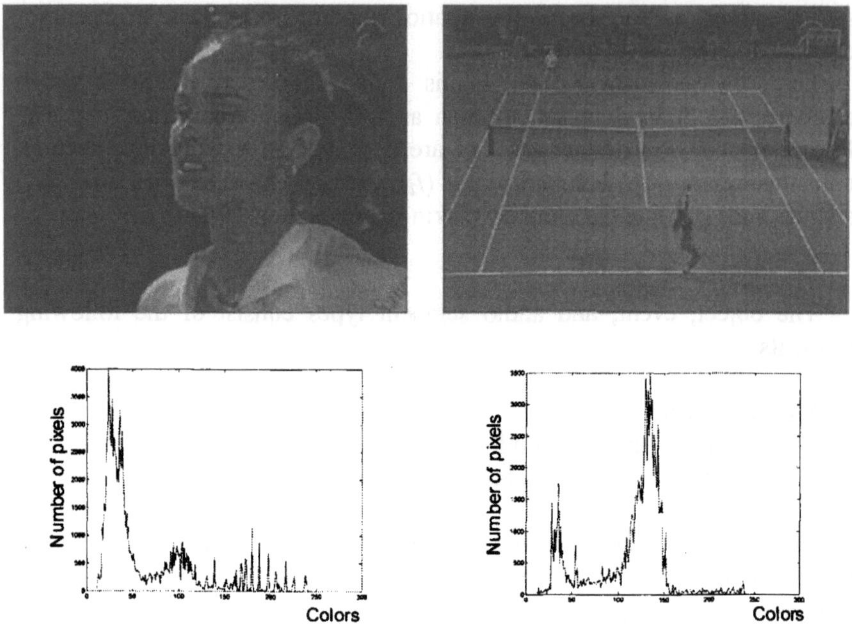

Figure 3.8. Color histograms of two frames belonging to different shots

The instances of objects, audio segments, and events are in the set O, AS, and E, respectively. Let us assume that some instances of the types defined in Σ_O, Σ_S, and Σ_E are extracted manually. The methods to automatically extract some other concepts from raw video data will be presented in the next chapters.

7. SUMMARY

This chapter is concerned with video modeling. It identifies differences between multimedia modeling and traditional data modeling taking into account requirements for content-based retrieval. In particular, a distinction is made between the modeling of the video structure and the modeling of the video content. The reason for the introduction of latter is that a video data model also has to include the concepts that represent the content of video, together with the elements that represent its inherent structural properties. These semantic concepts, as interpretation of the information that video conveys, allow a user to retrieve the video data based on content.

With regard to the modeling of the video content, two main groups of models founded in the literature are identified: feature-based models and annotation-based models. In order to overcome the drawbacks of both groups, a video modeling framework, called Cobra, is introduced. It integrates the two groups, supporting the automatic mapping of raw video data to features and subsequently to high-level concepts by integrating audio and video primitives. This gives the solid basis for building a content-based video retrieval system.

Instead of extending the basic feature-based retrieval with querying by keywords or captions, as in the Virage data model, the Cobra model is aiming at the automatic extraction of concepts (annotations) from visual features. For that purpose, the model is extended with an object and an event grammar, which will be described in the next chapter.

In this chapter, we have demonstrated on the real data from the Tennis case study how the video structure can be unfolded and given a meaning. This very simple video processing can be easily utilized if, for example, a user wants to see only the playing parts of a tennis match, or, on the other hand, only close-up or audience shots.

REFERENCES

[1] W. Grosky, "Managing Multimedia Information in Database Systems", *Communications of the ACM*, Vol. 40, No. 12, Dec. 1997, pp. 73-80.

[2] O. Marques, B. Furht, *Content-Based Image and Video Retrieval*, Kluwer Academic Publisher, 2002.

[3] J.S. Boreczky, L.A. Rowe, "Comparison of video shot boundary detection techniques", In *Proceedings SPIE Conference Storage and Retrieval for Video Databases IV*, San Jose, USA, 1995.

[4] H-J. Zhang, "Content-based Video Browsing and Retrieval" In *Handbook of Internet and Multimedia Systems and Applications* (B. Furht, ed.), CRC - IEEE Press, 1998.

[5] R. Brunelli, O. Mich, C. M. Modena, "A Survey on the Automatic Indexing of Video Data", *Journal of Visual Communication and Image Representation*, 10(2), pp. 78-112, 1999.

[6] B. Rubin, G. Davenport, "Structured Content Modeling for Cinematic Information", *SIGCHI Bulletin*, 21(2), 1989, pp.78-79.

[7] B-L. Yeo, M.M. Yeung, "Retrieving and Visualizing Video", *Communications of the ACM*, Vol. 40, No. 12, 1997, pp. 43-52.

[8] R. Weiss, A. Duda, D. K. Gifford, "Content-based Access to Algebraic Video", In *Proceedings of International Conference on Multimedia Computing and Systems*, IEEE Press, 1994, pp. 140-151.

[9] E. Oomoto, K. Tanaka, "OVID: Design and Implementation of a Video-Object Database System", *IEEE Transaction on Knowledge and Data Engineering*, Vol. 5, No. 4, Avgust, 1993, pp. 629-643.

[10] A. Hampapur, R. Jain, "Video Data Management Systems: Metadata and Architecture" in *Multimedia Data Management*, A. Sheth, W. Klas (ed.), McGraw-Hill, 1998.

[11] D. Swanberg, C.F. Shu, R. Jain, "Knowledge Guided Parsing in Video Databases", In *Proc. of SPIE Symposium on Electronic Imaging: Science and Technology*, February 1993, pp. 13-24.

[12] H. Zhang, S.W. Smoliar, "Developing Power Tools for Video Indexing and Retrieval", In *Proc. of SPIE Storage and Retrieval for Video Databases*, San Jose, CA, Jan. 1994.

[13] H. Wactlar, T. Kanade, M. Smith. S. Stevens, "Intelligent Access to Digital Video: Informedia Project", *IEEE Computer*, Vol. 4, No. 2, 1996.

[14] C. Snoek, M. Worring "A Review on Multimodal Video Indexing", In *the Proceedings of the IEEE International Conference on Multimedia and Expo (ICME)*, Lausanne, 2002.

[15] J. Z. Li, M. T. Ozsu, D. Szafron, "Modeling of Video Spatial Relationships in an Object Database Management System", In *Proceedings of International Workshop on Multimedia Database Management Systems*, 1996, pp. 124-132.

[16] M. Adiba, J.L. Zechinelli-Martini, "Managing Spatio-Temporal Multimedia Presentations as Database Objects", *Technical Report RR 1022-I-LSR 10*, IMAG, July 1999.

[17] P. Aigrain, H. Zhang, D. Petkovic, "Content-based Representation and Retrieval of Visual Media: A State-of-the-Art Review", *Multimedia Tools and Applications*, Kluwer Academic Publishers, 3(3), 1996, pp. 179-202.

[18] M. Petkovic, W. Jonker, "Overview of Data Models and Query Languages for Content-based Video Retrieval", *International Conference on Advances in Infrastructure for Electronic Business, Science, and Education on the Internet*, l'Aquila, Italy, 2000.

[19] A. Yoshitaka, T. Ichikawa, "A Survey on Content-Based Retrieval for Multimedia Databases", *IEEE Transactions on Knowledge and Data Engineering*, Vol. 11, No. 1, 1999, pp. 81-93.

[20] B. Perry, S-K. Chang, J. Dinsmore, D. Doermann, A. Rosenfeld, S. Stevens, *Content-based Access to Multimedia Information: From Technology Trends to State of the Art*, Kluwer Academic Publisher, 1999.

[21] J. R. Smith, S-F. Chang, "VisualSEEk: A Fully Automated Content-Based Image Query System", In *Proceedings of ACM Multimedia Conference*, Boston, MA, November 1996.

[22] A. Pentland, R. W. Picard, S. Sclaroff, "Photobook: Content-Based Manipulation of Image Databases", *International Journal of Computer Vision*, 18 (3), 1996, pp. 233-254.

[23] C. Nastar, M. Mitschke, C. Meilhac, N. Boujemaa, "Surfimage: A Flexible Content-Based Image Retrieval System", In *Proceedings of ACM Multimedia International Conference*, Bristol, England, 1998, pp. 339-344.

[24] C. Carson, M. Thomas, S. Belongie, J. M. Hellerstein, J. Malik, "Blobworld: A System for Region-Based Image Indexing and Retrieval", *Third International Conference on Visual Information and Information Systems*, Amsterdam, 1999, pp. 509-516.

[25] M. Flinker, H. S. Sawhney, W. Niblack, J. Ashley, Q. Huang, B. Dom, M. Gorkani, J. Hafner, D. N. Lee, D. Petkovic, D. Steele, P. Yanker, "Query by Image and Video Content: The QBIC System", *IEEE Computer*, 28, 1995, pp. 23-32.

[26] S-F. Chang, W. Chen, H. Meng, H. Sundaram, D. Zhong, "A Fully Automated Content Based Video Search Engine Supporting Spatio-Temporal Queries", *IEEE Transaction on Circuits and Systems for Video Technology*, Vol. 8, No. 5, Sept., 1998.

[27] A. Hampapur, A. Gupta, B. Horowitz, C-F. Shu, C. Fuller, J. Bach, M. Gorkani, R. Jain, "Virage Video Engine", In *Proceedings of SPIE* Vol. 3022, 1997.

[28] M. La Cascia, E. Ardizzone, "JACOB: Just a Content-based Query System for Video Databases", *Proceedings ICASSP-96*, Atlanta, GA, 1996, pp. 56-71.

[29] D. Ponceleon, S. Srinivasan, A. Amir, D. Petkovic, D. Diklic, "Key to Effective Video Retrieval: Effective Cataloging and Browsing", *ACM Multimedia*, 1998, pp. 99-107.

[30] W. Wolf, "Key Frame Selection by Motion Analysis", *Proceedings ICASSP-96*, Atlanta, GA, 1996.

[31] T. G. Aguierre Smith, G. Davenport, "The Stratification System: A Design Environment for Random Access Video", In *Proceedings of 3rd International Workshop on Network and operating system Support for Digital Audio and Video*, La Jolla, CA, 1992.

[32] S. Adali, K. S. Candan, S-S. Chen, K. Erol, V. S. Subrahmanian, "Advanced Video Information System: Data Structure and Query Processing", *Multimedia System*, Vol. 4, No. 4, Aug. 1996, pp. 172-86.

[33] C. Decleir, M-S. Hacid, J. Kouloumdjian, "A Database Approach for Modeling and Querying Video data", *LTCS-Report 99-03*, 1999.

[34] E. Ardizzone, M-S. Hacid, "A Semantic Modeling Approach for Video Retrieval by Content", In *Proceedings of the IEEE International Conference on Multimedia Computing and Systems*, Florence, Italy, June 1999.

[35] M. Davis, "Knowledge Representation for Video", *Proc. of 12th National Conference on Artificial Intelligence*, Vol. 1, Seattle, Washington, 1994, pp. 120-127.

[36] H. Jiang, A. Elmagarmid, "Spatial and temporal content-based access to hypervideo databases" *VLDB Journal*, 7(4), 1998, pp. 226-238.

[37] N. Dimitrova, F. Golshani, "Rx for Semantic Video Database Retrieval", In Proceedings of ACM Multimedia conference, 1994, pp. 219-226.

[38] A. Woudstra, D.D. Velthausz, H.J.G. de Poot, F. Moelaert El-Hadidy, W. Jonker, M.A.W. Houtsma, R.G. Heller, J.N.H. Heemskerk, "Modelling and Retrieving Audiovisual Information - A Soccer Video Retrieval System", *4th International Workshop on Multimedia Information Systems*; Istanbul, Turkey, September 1998.

[39] Y. Gong, L. T. Sin, C. H. Chuan, H-J. Zhang, M. Sakauchi, "Automatic Parsing of TV Soccer Programs", In *Proceedings of IEEE International Conference on Multimedia Computing and Systems*, Washington D. C., 1995, pp. 167-174.

[40] S. Intille, A. Bobick, "Visual Tracking Using Closed-Worlds", *M.I.T. Media Laboratory Technical Report* No. 294, Nov. 1994.

[41] G. P. Pingali, Y. Jean I. Carlbom, "LucentVision: A System for Enhanced Sports Viewing", In *Proceedings of Visual'99 International Conference*, Amsterdam, 1999, pp. 689-696.

[42] F. Golshani, N. Dimitrova, "A Language for Content-Based Video Retrieval", *Multimedia Tools and Applications*, 6 (3), 1998, pp. 289-312.

[43] M. Petkovic, W. Jonker, "A Framework for Video Modeling", *In Proceedings of Eighteenth IASTED International Conference on Applied Informatics*, Innsbruck, February 2000, pp. 317-322.

[44] MPEG Requirements Group, *MPEG-7 visual part of eXperimentation Model 6.0*, ISO/IEC JTC1/SC29/WG11 MPEG2000/N3398, Geneva, CH, June 2000.

[45] MPEG Requirements Group, *Working Draft 2.0 of MPEG-7 Visual*, ISO/IEC JTC1/SC29/WG11 MPEG2000 N3322, Noordwijkerhout, NL, March 2000.

[46] J.S. Boreczky, L.A. Rowe, "Comparison of video shot boundary detection techniques", In *Proceedings of SPIE Conference Storage and Retrieval for Video Databases IV*, San Jose, USA, 1995.

[47] M. Petkovic, *Content-Based Video Retrieval Supported by Database Technology*, PhD Thesis, Centre for Telematics and Information Technology Ph.D. Thesis Series No. 02-48, Enschede, the Netherlands, 2003.

Chapter 4

SPATIO-TEMPORAL FORMALIZATION OF VIDEO EVENTS

1. INTRODUCTION

As concluded in the previous chapter, the main gap in video retrieval lies between the low-level media features and the high-level concepts. However, as video is a temporal sequence of pixel regions at the physical level, it is very difficult to explore its semantic content. To solve this problem, several domain-dependent research efforts have been undertaken. These approaches take advantage of using domain knowledge to facilitate extraction of high-level concepts directly from features. In particular, they mainly use information on object positions, their transitions over time, and relate them to particular events (high-level concepts). For example, methods have been proposed to detect events in football games [1], soccer games [2], tennis [3, 4], hunting [5], events in a static room [6], etc. Motion (for a review see [7]) and audio are, in isolation, very often used for event recognition. In [8] for example, the extraction of highlights from baseball games is based on audio only.

Although these efforts resulted in an automatic extraction of video events from raw data, the mentioned approaches are limited on a specific domain, because the mapping is hard-coded in the system and impossible either to fine-tune or change. In addition, majority of these methods are not extensible for detecting new events because they are very dependent on specific artifacts used in the broadcasts of domain programs.

In this chapter, we describe the extension of the Cobra framework, which aims at formalizing descriptions of high-level concepts, as well as at facilitating their extraction based on features and spatio-temporal reasoning. In contrast to the approaches mentioned above, which mainly come from the computer vision community, having often scalability problems, we address the problem from the database point of view. Consequently, our approach aims at a more general solution that can be used in different domains. The extended framework provides the basis for the system that will allow users to dynamically define and query new multimedia objects and events.

The remainder of this chapter is organized as follows. The next section defines an extension of the Cobra framework, which involves an object and an event grammar, as well as some necessary operators. In Section 3, we revisit the Tennis case study to illustrate the potential of the framework extension with respect to interpreting video features into semantic content. Along with examples of spatio-temporal formalization of high-level concepts, it describes a player segmentation and tracking algorithm, as well as a feature extraction process. Section 4 summarizes the work presented in this chapter.

2. SPATIO-TEMPORAL EXTENSION OF THE COBRA FRAMEWORK

In order to facilitate automatic extraction of concepts (objects and events) from visual features, the Cobra framework, which is introduced in the previous chapter, has been extended with an object and an event grammar. The grammars are aimed at formalizing descriptions of high-level concepts, based on feature and spatio-temporal relations. Therefore, we introduce the following three elements in the extension of our video modeling framework: G_O, G_E, and α.

G_O is an object grammar. It defines the syntax that is used for object type descriptions. Object types can be primitive or compound. If we look at the soccer domain, for example, a goalpost can be seen as a primitive object type that is composed of two regions, i.e. white bars and a net. These regions are homogeneous in certain features and several spatial relations exist between them. Despite the fact that objects are defined as entities with a prominent spatial dimension, we take advantage of temporality, allowing the usage of temporal relations in the formalizations of object descriptions. In this way, some temporal properties of objects can be used along spatial properties to enhance object extraction and make it more robust.

Compound objects consist of two or more primitive ones. For example, the goalpost object can also be defined as a compound object if the white bars and the net are previously defined as separate objects. The formalization of object and event descriptions is facilitated by a graphical user interface, which will be described in Chapter 6. In order to help understanding the examples given at the end of this chapter, we introduce the following notation for the formalizations of object type descriptions:

$\rho_{Oprimitive}$: $(o_1, o_2, o_3, o_4, o_5) \rightarrow o$, $\rho_{Ocompound}$: $(o_6, o_3, o_4, o_5) \rightarrow o$,

where o_1 is a subset of the set VS, $o_2 \subseteq \Sigma_S$, $o_6 \subseteq \Sigma_O$, and $o \in O$. The set o_3 consists of the expressions of the following type: $\vartheta(\upsilon_1, \upsilon_2)$ or $\vartheta(\upsilon_1)$ where ϑ is a feature operation from the set φ, while υ_1 and υ_2 are elements of the sets VS or AS. The same holds for o_4 and o_5, where operations are from the set σ and the set τ, respectively. The sets of feature operators, spatial, and temporal relations (φ, σ, and τ respectively), which are used in the object formalizations, will be explained later in this section.

Note that instead of the object grammar, it is also possible to use other techniques for object recognition. For example, objects can be extracted by specific external algorithms for object recognition, such as the one described in [9]. Another example is our tennis player detector, which will be described later when we come back to the Tennis case study. On the other hand, the framework can also make use of objects that are already defined in an MPEG4 video stream [10].

G_E is an event grammar. It consists of formalizations that are used for event type descriptions. Similar to the object types, event types can be primitive or compound. Two different formalizations of primitive event types exist. The first one defines events using visual features and their spatio-temporal and similarity relations, whereas the second one uses object types instead of features, together with their domain (conceptual) relations (ω). Audio segment types may also be included. Hence, it is possible to define audio events and compound audio-visual events. On the other hand, a compound event type is described by a subset of predefined event types, their temporal relations, as well as real-world and spatial relations among their objects. The event formalizations have the following three different forms:

$\rho_{Eprimitve\_VS}$: $(e_1, e_2, e_3, e_4, e_5) \rightarrow e$, $\rho_{Eprimitve\_O}$: $(e_6, e_2, e_7, e_4, e_5) \rightarrow e$,

$\rho_{Ecompound}$: $(e_8, e_2, e_7, e_4, e_5) \rightarrow e$,

where e_1 is a subset of the set VS, $e_2 \subseteq \Sigma_S$, $e_6 \subseteq \Sigma_O$, $e_8 \subseteq \Sigma_E$, and $e \in E$. The set e_3 consists of the expressions of the following type: $\vartheta(\upsilon_1, \upsilon_2)$ or $\vartheta(\upsilon_1)$ where ϑ is a feature operation from φ, while υ_1 and υ_2 are elements of VS or AS. The same holds for e_4, e_5, and e_7, where operations are from the set σ, τ, and ω, respectively, and operands are elements of the set Σ_O.

The last element in the spatio-temporal extension of our framework is the set of algebraic operators, denoted by α. It includes sets of spatial, temporal, feature, domain relationships and so-called video operators, i.e. $\alpha = \{\sigma, \tau, \varphi, \omega, \upsilon\}$. These operators are described in the following three subsections.

2.1 Spatial relations

Spatial relations include topological, directional, and distance relations. Topological relations describe concepts of neighborhood and stay invariant under transformations such as translation, rotation, and scaling. Direction relations deal with order in space. A notion of distance between points help us to define circles or spheres around points and thereby neighborhoods of points. The most often used metric is the Euclidian metric.

In video documents, we mainly deal with contiguous regions, i.e. homogeneously 2-dimensional connected objects with connected boundaries, as defined by the 9-intersection model [11]. According to this model, each object is represented in two-dimensional space as a point set, which has an interior, a boundary, and an exterior. The topological relations between any two objects are described by the nine intersections of the three properties of each of two objects. Although 512 different relations can be distinguished by the model, only the following eight are meaningful for region objects [12]: disjoint, meet, equal, overlap, contains, inside, covers, and covered_by.

A geometric representation of a video object is one of the challenging problems. A polygonal representation is very accurate and indispensable for precise topological constraint evaluation. However, it is a common strategy when dealing with spatial objects to use approximations of the object geometry to increase efficiency. Although there are several options in choosing object approximations, the Minimum Bounding Rectangle (MBR) approximation has been used most extensively. The reason is that it needs only two points for its representation (one corresponding to the lower left and another to the upper right corner of the MBR). However, MBRs show some disadvantages when dealing with non-convex or diagonal objects.

If we look at relations between two MBRs, represented by two points, then the number of relations in one-dimensional space is 13 (Figure 4.1). These relations correspond to the relations between time intervals defined by Allen [13], which will be described in the next section. If we look at two-dimensional space, there are 169 (13 square) different configurations [14], which are shown in Figure 4.2. By mapping the configurations to eight topological relations, we can conclude that the total number of configurations in which MBRs are overlapped are 50, 48 correspond to the disjoint relation, 40 to meet, 14 to covers and covered_by, and only one to equal, contains, and inside.

Figure 4.1. Relations between two MBRs in one-dimensional space

Figure 4.2. Relations between two MBRs in two-dimensional space (1 – disjoint, 2 – meet, 3 – overlap, 4 – covers, 5 – covered_by, 6 – inside, 7 – equal, 8 – contains)

The eight topological relations, disjoint, overlap, meet, equal, inside, covers, and covered_by, denoted with numbers in Figure 4.2, are elements of the set σ and as such are used in the spatio-temporal extension of the Cobra framework.

The directional relations, which we use, are based on the cone-shaped concept of directions. In other words, they are defined using angular regions between objects, which are abstracted as single points based on the center of mass. We defined eight directional relations (north, south, west, east, north-east, north-west, south-east, and south-west), similarly to the work of Peuquet and Ci-Xiang [15], which involves only four relations (north, east, west, and south). The set σ is extended with these eight directional relations.

As far as a distance relation is concerned let us first discuss a generalization of the notion of the Euclidian distance. A function d: $M \times M \rightarrow R$, where M denotes a set and R the set of positive real numbers, is called a metric on M, if the following conditions are fulfilled for all x, y, z $\in$ M:

- $d(x, y) \geq 0$, and $d(x, y) = 0 \Leftrightarrow x = y$,
- $d(x, y) = d(y, x)$,
- $d(x, y) + d(y, z) \geq d(x, z)$.

The first property ensures that there is no negative distance of points, while the second guarantees that the distance between two points is the same regardless of whether we measure from x to y or from y to x. The third property is the triangular inequality. The Euclidean metric, we use in the Cobra extension, is defined as follows:

$$M = R^2 : d(x, y) = \sqrt{\sum_{i=1}^{2} (x_i - y_i)^2} .$$

Extension to n-dimensional space is straightforward. Some other metric examples are given in the following:

$$M = R^3 : d(x, y) = \sum_{i=1}^{3} |x_i - y_i| ,$$

$M = R^3 : d(x, y) = 0$, if $x = y$, and $d(x, y) = 1$ if not.

$M = R^2 : d(x, y) = | x_1 - y_1 |$

$M = R^2 : d(x, y) = | x_2 - y_2 |$

We also use the last two metrics in our framework. Throughout this book they are denoted by 'x distance' and 'y distance', respectively. Note that qualitative distance relations, such as 'near' and 'far', can also be defined.

2.2 Temporal relations

Video elements (usually shots) can be identified by basic time units, which can be either time instants or time intervals. Qualitative relations between temporal objects are well defined. They can be categorized in the point temporal algebra or interval temporal algebra [16]. The point algebra uses time instant as a primitive object. Time instants are zero-length moments in time. Three basic relations (<, =, >) are defined between two objects. Temporal intervals consist of time durations bounded by two endpoints - time instants. The relative relations between two time intervals can be determined from their endpoints. There are thirteen different ways[1] in which two intervals can be related. All thirteen relations can be represented by the following seven: *before, meets, overlaps, during, starts, finishes, equal*. The other six are inverse relations. For example, '*after*' (Figure 4.1, relation R_{13}) is the inverse relation of '*before*' (Figure 4.1, relation R_1). Only the equality relation has no inverse. We refer to [13] for a formal definition of the temporal relations. Time instant relations can be considered as a special case of time interval relations, where a time interval has the same bounds, or vice versa, relations between two intervals with denoted bounds can be expressed by time instant relations.

The seven temporal relations τ = {*before, meets, overlaps, during, starts, finishes, equal*} are included in the spatio-temporal extension of the Cobra framework. To provide a precise timing, we add a parameter to the three of these temporal relations: *before (A, B, n)*, *overlaps (A, B, n)*, and *during (A, B, n)*. Symbols A and B denote time intervals and *n* denotes the time difference between the starting point of A and the starting point of B in the case of the *before* relation, but duration of overlapping in the case of the *overlaps* and *during* relations (see Figure 4.3).

Note that based on all these operations new ones can be defined to enhance the power of spatial and temporal relations. These operations could be used to model the temporal changing of object's x and y co-ordinates, as well as to model the object's trajectory. As an example, a set of video operations called modifiers is defined in [17]. The authors defined Increasing, Decreasing and Equal modifier to specify the variance of spatial relationships.

[1] They correspond to the relations between two MBRs in one-dimensional space, shown in Figure 4.1

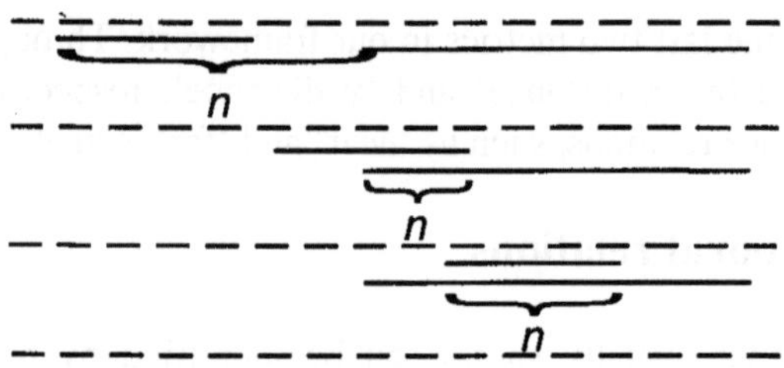

Figure 4.3. Precise timing with three interval relations

2.3 Feature, domain, and video operators

The set of feature operators φ is used for feature extraction and similarity matching. It consists of operators that deal with color, texture, shape, and motion. For example, the color part consists of operators that extract features such as: color space, dominant color, color histogram, color quantization, group of frames color histogram, color-structure histogram, color layout, and compact color descriptor. The other features, characterizing texture, shape, and motion are listed in the MPEG-7 standard [18, 19]. This document also describes the algorithms for extraction of these features, as well as similarity matching criteria.

The set of conceptual relations ω is domain dependent. For the tennis domain, it can comprise relations like 'is_right_handed', 'plays_closer_to_camera', etc. These relations can have a temporal dimension, so they can be related to a specific time interval. The set of video operators υ consists of operations on video frames and segments: *creation*, *concatenation*, *union*, *intersection*, *difference*, and *s_contains*. The last one checks if objects or events are present in a sequence, while others enable interpretation, composition, and manipulation of video segments.

3. TENNIS CASE STUDY REVISITED

The spatio-temporal formalization of video events is validated using three case studies that have been set up during the development of the method. They were from a medical and a sport domain. The medical case study deals with gait modeling, defining some walking problems like walking on toes, wide walking, etc. In the sport domain, we have two case studies, one in the soccer and an extensive one in the tennis domain. The soccer case study describes formalizations for events such as 'player has a ball', 'cheering', 'scoring a goal', etc. The descriptions of the soccer and the gait modeling case study can be found in [20].

The examples given in this chapter are from the Tennis case study. Experiments in this case study are based on ordinary TV broadcast videos with different players at different tournaments: Australian Open, Swisscom Challenge, Vienna Open, etc. They are intended to show how the spatio-temporal approach can be used to map features into high-level concepts in the tennis domain. The aim was to automatically extract events like net-playing, rally, longest point, and shortest point from tennis videos.

The entire process of tennis video analysis is shown in Figure 4.4. In the previous chapter, we have already described the shot detection and classification process, which allows us to select only playing shots from the whole tennis game video. Here, we concentrate on these playing shots and demonstrate how the player can be segmented and tracked. First, we explain an algorithmic solution for an external object extractor, while we also give a solution that uses the object grammar of our framework to accomplish the same task. Next, the features that are extracted from the segmented shape of a player are briefly explained and listed. Finally, our leading example is updated with new features, which are used together with spatio-temporal relations to extract desired events.

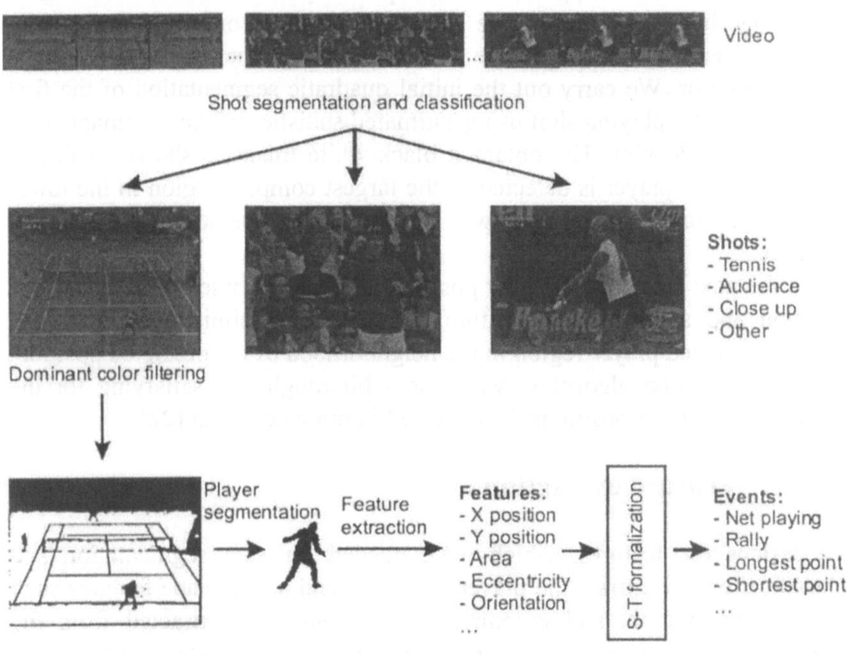

Figure 4.4. Tennis video analysis

Figure 4.5. Player segmentation: (a) Original image; (b) Initial segmentation

3.1 Player segmentation and tracking

Our analysis concentrates on the playing shots (camera observing the whole field as in Figure 4.5a). Hindered by the low quality of the video and trying to make a clear approach not hampered by a large amount of domain knowledge heuristics needed, we constrain ourselves only to the player in the lower part of the image. The first step of segmentation is to filter the dominant color. We carry out the initial quadratic segmentation of the first two images of a playing shot using estimated statistics of the dominant color (see [21] for details). The obtained black-white image is shown in Figure 4.5b. Then, the player is detected as the largest compact region in the lower half of the image using the two morphological operations erosion and dilation.

In the next frames, the player position is predicted based on the previous position and speed. The algorithm searches for a similar region to the initially detected player region in the neighborhood of the predicted position. This segmentation algorithm, which is a bit rough, but satisfying for the extraction of player positions, is described in more details in [22].

3.2 Feature extraction

Besides the features, which were needed for shot segmentation and classification, we extract the player's position and a few shape features such as area, orientation, and eccentricity. The latter are extracted from the segmented binary representation of the player. The complete list of features is: color histogram (f_1)[2], dominant color (f_2), entropy characteristics mean (f_3) and variance (f_4), number of skin colored pixels (f_5), player's position (f_6), area (f_7), orientation (f_8), and eccentricity (f_9).

The center of mass of the region is taken as the player position. Area denotes the actual number of pixels in the region. Eccentricity is the eccentricity of the ellipse that has the same second-moment as the region (see Figure 4.6). It is the ratio of the distance between the foci of the ellipse and its major axis length (e = c/a). The eccentricity takes the value between zero and one, which are actually degenerate cases. An ellipse with the eccentricity zero is a circle, while an ellipse with the eccentricity one is a line segment. Orientation is the angle between the x-axis and the major axis of the ellipse that has the same second-moment as the region (α in Figure 4.6).

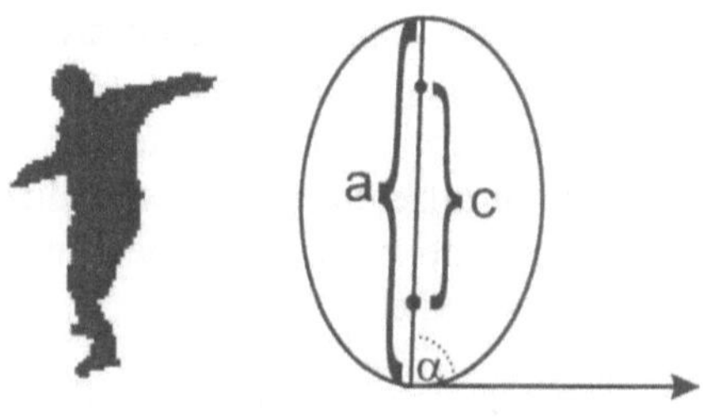

Figure 4.6. Eccentricity and orientation

3.3 Spatio-temporal formalization of tennis video events

In this section, we continue with our modeling example. With the analysis presented in this chapter, the set of feature types is expanded to include the mentioned shape features:

$$\Sigma_F = \{f_1, f_2, f_3, f_4, f_5, f_6, f_7, f_8, f_9\}$$

Chapter 3 established the following high-level concepts, which are assumed to be already defined and extracted:

Σ_O = {ball, net}
Σ_S = {cheering, stroke_sound, sigh_sound}
Σ_E = {service, volley, ace, player_near_the_base-line}

[2] Note that this is not only one value, but 256 values. For simplicity, we will denote this as only one feature. This also holds for a few more features.

In the remainder of this section, we first give some examples of primitive object and event descriptions based on only extracted features and then present some more examples of compound event descriptions that build on already defined descriptions.

Video objects can be extracted using the domain knowledge accumulated in the descriptions of the object grammar. For example, a primitive object description that extracts the player closer to the camera from a segmented playing shot using shape features and the spatial relation *contain* is defined as:

ρ_{Player}: ({r_1: body, r_2: rect(0, 144, 384, 288)}, {$700 < f_7(r_1) < 1200$}, {contain(r_2, r_1)}, {}).

There are two regions involved: r_1 corresponds to the player and r_2 to the lower part of the frame. The criteria concerning the area feature (f_7) has to be fulfilled. Furthermore, the region r_2 has to contain the region r_1.

Nevertheless, different descriptions can be used for the extraction of the same object. They can rely on different features and different granularity of segmentation. The following one uses more specific features assuming a finer segmentation of player's shape:

ρ_{Player} : ({r_1:body, r_2:dress, r_3, r_4 :leg}, {}, {$700<f_7(r_1)<1200$, $f_2(r_2) = 256$, $f_3(r_3) + f_5(r_4) > 20$, $0.7 < f_9(r_1) < 1$}, {touch(r_2, r_3), touch(r_2, r_4)}, {})

Let us look at some primitive event descriptions. The first example would retrieve all video segments where Venus Williams is playing close to the net for a given period of time.

$\rho_{Player\_near\_the\_net}$: ({o_1: player, o_2: net}, { o_1.name = 'V.Williams' },{}, {y_distance (o_1, o_2) < 50}, {duration > 60})

The new "player_near_the_net" event type is defined in terms of spatio-temporal object interactions assuming that objects like player and net have been already extracted. This description also shows how event types can be parameterized (a user might be interested not only in Venus Williams, but in different players playing close to the net). However, in order to make use of conceptual data, the name has to be linked to the player's shape already in the process of visual analysis. For the distinction between Venus Williams and Martina Hingis, for example, a user intervention in the process of annotation is needed, or some other techniques might be used to determine the difference automatically. To accomplish that automatically, one can use the superimposed text that supplements visual information. Namely, the beginning sequences of a tennis match usually contain the superimposed text with names of both players. The text with the name of a player is placed next to that player as shown in Figure 4.7.

Therefore, the players can be distinguished using a video OCR technique together with some visual analysis. The features, such as color histogram or dominant color of the region containing a player, can be extracted from the frames that contain the superimposed names of players. The player's name is recognized using a video OCR technique. Then, the extracted features can be associated with the player's name. In the remaining frames of the video, which do not have the superimposed text, a player can be automatically recognized based on its visual features. More details about text detection and recognition will be given in Chapter 5.

Let us go back and consider the description of the event type 'Player near the net'. There are two types of objects involved the player and the net. There are no audio types, but there is a constraint on a domain attribute, one spatial relation (*distance*) defined on player's position (feature f_6), and also one temporal relation (*duration*). The temporal relation says that this event type should last for a specific period, as well as that the spatial relation should be valid for that period of time. In the sequel, we introduce some other primitive event descriptions:

$\rho_{Forehand\_touch}$: ({o_1:player, o_2:ball}, {stroke_sound}, {is_right-handed(o_1), playing_closer_to_camera(o_1)}, {overlap(o_1, o_2), east(o_2, o_1)}, { })

$\rho_{Backhand\_touch}$: ({o_1:player, o_2:ball}, {stroke_sound}, {is_right-handed(o_1), playing_closer_to_camera(o_1)}, {overlap(o_1, o_2), west(o_2, o_1)}, { })

$\rho_{Ball\_is\_free}$: ({o_1, o_2 :player, o_3:ball}, {}, {}, {distance(o_1, o_3) > 10, distance(o_2, o_3) > 10}, { })

The first two define forehand- and backhand-touch events based on some conceptual information about the player and the topological operator overlap and direction operators east and west, which ensure that the ball is on the right side of the player. The third description is for the event ball-is-free. Note that this formalization takes into consideration only two dimensions of a 3-dimensional event. For a more accurate description, a 3D model of the scene is needed (as it will be introduced in Chapter 5).

A user can also reuse already defined event types in order to define compound ones. For example, in our case study the rally event is defined as a compound event. First, we define primitive events Player_in_the-right_corner and Player_in_the_left_corner:

$\rho_{Player\_in\_right\_corner}$: ({o_1:player}, { }, {f_6.x(o_1) > 190, f_6.y(o_1) > 170}, { }, { })

$\rho_{Player\_in\_left\_corner}$: ({o_1:player}, { }, {f_6.x(o_1) < 190, f_6.y(o_1) > 170}, { }, { })

Having these two events formalized one can create a compound event type that can be used to extract all frame sequences in which a player goes two times from the left part of the court to the right part and back. This event is called left-to-right rally.

$\rho_{LtRRally}$: ({e_1,e_2:player_in_left_corner, e_3,e_4:player_in_right_corner}, {$e_1.o_1 = e_2.o_1 = e_3.o_1 = e_4.o_1$}, {}, {meet($e_1$, e_3), meet(e_3, e_2) , meet(e_2, e_4)}})

So, based on primitive event formalizations a user can build new events. The list of described events grows very quickly. For example, in the following event description, possible lobs are retrieved by describing a new event type using the already defined events ('Player_near_the_net' and 'Player_near_the_base-line') and some additional criteria (the interval relation *meets* means that event e_1 has to finish at the same moment when e_2 starts).

ρ_{Lob} : ({e_1: player_near_the_net, e_2: player_near_the_base-line}, { $e_1.o_1 = e_2.o_1$}, {}, {meet (e_1, e_2)}})

However, this query will not retrieve all lobs (for example, the ones where the player stays at the net or smash the ball at the service line). To be able to retrieve all lobs, the position of the ball must be determined.

Using the primitive events defined above, one can define more compound events such as the 'Forehand' and 'Service-volley' events. These formalizations use the position of the ball.

$\rho_{Forehand}$: ({e_1:forehand_touch, e_2, e_3:ball_is_free}, { }, {}, {meet(e_2, e_1), meet(e_1, e_3)})

$\rho_{Service\text{-}Volley}$: ({e_1:service, e_2, e_3:ball_is_free, e_4:return, e_5:volley}, {$e_1.o_1$ = $e_5.o_1$, $e_1.o_1$!= $e_4.o_1$}, {}, {meet(e_1, e_2), meet(e_2, e_4) , meet(e_4, e_3) , meet(e_3 e_5)})

For a naïve user, it might be very difficult to create an object or event description, especially when it comes to the formalization of complex actions of non-rigid objects involving many objects and features. In order to simplify the process of describing these semantic concepts, a graphical user interface is developed. It is presented together with our prototype of a video retrieval system in Chapter 6.

4. SUMMARY

In order to bridge the gap in content-based video retrieval, which lies between low-level media features and high-level concepts, a spatio-temporal formalization of video events has been introduced. The Cobra framework has been extended with object and event grammars that support automatic extraction of concepts (objects and events) from visual features. The grammars define the syntax that is used for creating the object and event type descriptions based on features and spatio-temporal relations.

The spatio-temporal formalization of video events has been demonstrated using the Tennis case study. First, a tennis video has been segmented into shots, which are classified in four different categories: playing, close-up, audience, and other. Then the focus has been moved to the playing shots, where the player closer to camera has been extracted and tracked.

Finally, having the features and objects extracted, the case study shows how the spatio-temporal and feature relations used by the object and the event grammar can be employed to map features into high-level concepts in the tennis domain. Thanks to that, events like net-playing, rally, and lob can be automatically extracted from tennis videos. In Chapter 6, we elaborate more on that describing the implementation of a real system and presenting some query examples.

REFERENCES

[1] S. Intille, A. Bobick, "Visual Tracking Using Closed-Worlds", *Tech. Report No. 294*, M.I.T. Media Laboratory, 1994.

[2] Y. Gong, L. T. Sin, C. H. Chuan, H-J. Zhang, M. Sakauchi, "Automatic Parsing of TV Soccer Programs", In *Proceedings of the IEEE International Conference on Multimedia Computing and Systems*, Washington D.C., 1995, pp. 167-174.

[3] H. Miyamori, S-I. Iisaku, "Video Annotation for Content-based Retrieval using Human Behavior Analysis and Domain Knowledge", In *Proc. of the IEEE International Conference on Automatic Face and Gesture Recognition*, Grenoble, France, 2000, pp. 320-325.

[4] G. Sudhir, J. Lee, A. Jain, "Automatic Classification of Tennis Video for High-level Content-based Retrieval", *IEEE Workshop on Content-based Access and Image and Video Databases*, Bombay, India, 1998, pp. 81-90.

[5] N. Haering, R.J. Qian, M.I. Sezan, "A semantic event-detection approach and its application to detecting hunts in wildlife video", *Circuits and Systems for Video Technology, IEEE Transactions on*, 10(6), Sept. 2000, pp. 857-868.

[6] D. Ayers, M. Shah, "Recognizing Human Actions in a Static Room", *IEEE Workshop on Applications of Computer Vision (WACV)*, Princeton, NJ, 1998, pp. 42-47.

[7] M. Shah, R. Jain (eds), *Motion-Based Recognition*, Kluwer Academic Publishers, 1997.

[8] Y. Rui, A. Gupta, A. Acero, "Automatically Extracting Highlights for TV Baseball Programs", In *Proceedings of the ACM Multimedia International Conference*, Los Angeles, CA, 2000, pp. 105-115.

[9] D. A. Forsyth, J. Malik, M. M. Fleck, H. Greenspan, T. Leung, S. Belongie, C. Carson, C. Bregler, "Finding Pictures of Objects in Large Collections of Images", In *the Proceedings of European Conference on Computer Vision (ECCV) '96 Workshop on Object Representation*, Cambridge, April 1996.

[10] International Organization for Standardization, *Overview of the MPEG-4 Standard*, R. Koenen (ed), N2995, Melbourne, October 1999.

[11] M. Egenhofer, "Reasoning about Binary Topological Relations", In *the Proceedings of the Second Symposium on the Design and Implementation of Large Spatial Databases*, Springer Verlag LNCS.

[12] M. Egenhofer, R. Franzosa, "Point-set topological spatial relations", *International Journal of Geographic Information Systems*, Vol. 5, No. 2, pp. 161-174.

[13] J. F. Allen, "Maintaining knowledge about temporal intervals", *Communications of ACM*, 26(11), 1983, pp. 832-843.

[14] D. Papadias, Y. Theodoridis, T. Sellis, and M. Egenhofer, "Topological Relations in the World of Minimum Bounding Rectangles: A Study with R-Trees", *SIGMOD RECORD* 24 (2), 1995, pp. 92-103.

[15] D. Peuquet, Z. Ci-Xiang, "An Algorithm to Determine the Directional Relationship between Arbitrarily-Shaped Polygons in the Plane", *Pattern Recognition*, Vol. 20, No. 1, pp 65-74.

[16] H-J. Chang, S-K. Chang, "Temporal Modeling and Intermedia Synchronization for Presentation of Multimedia Streams", In *Multimedia Information Storage and Management*, S. M. Chung (ed.), Kluwer Academic Publishers, 1996, pp. 373-398.

[17] T. C.T. Kuo, A. L.P. Chen, "A Content-Based Query Language for Video Databases", *Proc. of IEEE Multimedia Computing Systems*, 1996.

[18] MPEG Requirements Group, *MPEG-7 visual part of eXperimentation Model 6.0*, ISO/IEC JTC1/SC29/WG11 MPEG2000/N3398, Geneva, CH, June 2000.

[19] MPEG Requirements Group, *Working Draft 2.0 of MPEG-7 Visual*, ISO/IEC JTC1/SC29/WG11 MPEG2000 N3322, Noordwijkerhout, NL, March 2000.

[20] M. Petkovic, W. Jonker, "A Framework for Video Modeling", *In Proceedings of Eighteenth IASTED International Conference on Applied Informatics*, Innsbruck, February 2000, pp. 317-322.

[21] Z. Zivkovic, F. van der Heijden, M. Petkovic, W. Jonker, "Image processing and feature extraction for recognizing strokes in tennis game videos", In *the Proceedings of the Seventh Annual Conference of the Advanced School for Computing and Imaging*, the Netherlands, June 2001.

[22] M. Petkovic, R. Zwol, H. E. Blok, W. Jonker, P. M. G. Apers, M. Windhouwer, M. Kersten, "Content-based Video Indexing for the Support of Digital Library Search", In *Proceedings of 18th IEEE International Conference on Data Engineering (ICDE)*, San Jose, USA, February 2002.

Chapter 5

STOCHASTIC MODELING OF VIDEO EVENTS

1. INTRODUCTION

Although we have demonstrated in the previous chapter that spatio-temporal formalization can be used for inferring video semantics from low-level feature representations and extracting events like net-playing and rally, the presented approach has some drawbacks. Firstly, it is essentially restricted to the extent of recognizable events, since it might become difficult to formalize complex actions of non-rigid objects using the proposed approach. This especially holds for an ordinary user who is not familiar with video features and spatio-temporal reasoning. An expert can help, but even then for some events the approach will not grant the best results. If we consider the tennis strokes for example, one can argue that they can be formalized like in the last section of the previous chapter. However, that will not result in reasonable accuracy (see [1] for example). On the other hand, introducing the ball position and some other features in the event descriptions might increase the accuracy, but unfortunately, it will make these descriptions too complicated. Furthermore, it is very difficult to find and track the ball because of its high speed (can be more than 200km/h) and occlusion problems. Finally, the proposed approach requires that someone, either a user or an expert, creates object and event descriptions, which can be time-consuming and error-prone.

In order to overcome the above mentioned drawbacks, we propose the use of stochastic techniques, such as Hidden Markov Models (HMMs) and Bayesian belief networks. These techniques often exploit automatic learning capabilities to derive knowledge and avoid the need for an expert. Moreover, these stochastic techniques have been successfully used for similar problems in speech recognition and recognition of human actions and gestures. The first publication addressing recognition of human actions using HMMs [2] describes the application of discrete HMMs in recognizing six different tennis stroke classes in a constrained test environment. Recently, similar techniques have been proposed. Naphade et al. [3] used hierarchical HMMs to extract events like explosions. Mitrovic [4] described the application of HMMs for driving event recognition. HMMs together with a Bayesian classifier have been used for recognition of human actions in [5]. Structuring of video using Bayesian Networks alone [6] or together with HMMs [7] has been proposed as well.

Numerous approaches presented in the literature have shown that it is now becoming possible to extract high-level semantic events from a video. However, the greater part of them is constrained by a limited domain and a specific test environment. For example, Yamato et al. [2] consider recognition of tennis strokes in a specific test environment using close-up scenes of people performing strokes in front of a known background.

Furthermore, the majority of the aforementioned approaches uses the individual visual or audio cues, and therefore is error-prone suffering from robustness problems due to detection errors. According to the current understanding of human perception, it is expected that using the evidence obtained from different information sources should result in a more robust and accurate perception of computer systems. Moreover, some events are naturally multi-modal demanding the gathering of evidence from different media sources. On the other hand, the fusion of the multi-modal evidence is quite challenging for computer, since it has to deal with indications obtained from different media information sources, which might contradict each other. Only a few attempts to fuse mainly audio and video sources in order to detect and recognize events have appeared recently. In [8] a probabilistic model has been used to combine results of visual and audio event detection in order to identify topics of discussion in a classroom lecture environment. Another probabilistic framework that comprises multimedia objects within a Bayesian multinet has been proposed in [9]. A Bayesian approach for topic segmentation and classification in TV programs has been described in [10].

Bearing in mind the aforementioned facts, this chapter focuses on Hidden Markov Models (HMMs) and Bayesian Networks (BNs) and demonstrates how they can be effectively used for content-based video retrieval. We investigate the practical exploitation of HMMs in a real situation using the ordinary TV broadcast of tennis matches [11]. On the other hand, we also analyze the use of Bayesian networks for multi-modal content-based video retrieval. This approach is validated in the particular domain of Formula 1 race videos [12]. For both the Tennis and Formula 1 domain, we introduce robust audio-visual feature extraction schemes and a text recognition and detection method. Based on numerous experiments performed with Bayesian networks, we give some recommendations with respect to the modeling of temporal dependences and different learning algorithms.

The remainder of this chapter is organized as follows. The next two sections are introductory sections that give some theoretical background of hidden Markov models and Bayesian networks. Section 4 is dedicated to the Tennis case study, i.e. to the recognition of tennis strokes using hidden Markov models. The extraction of highlights from Formula 1 race videos using Bayesian and Dynamic Bayesian Networks (DBNs) is described in Section 5. The last section summarizes the chapter bringing some conclusions.

2. HIDDEN MARKOV MODELS

As very effective tools for modeling time-varying patterns, HMMs have been successfully applied in many fields, such as speech recognition, and more recently in human gesture recognition and handwriting recognition. Another reason for their wide applications comes from their self-organizing learning capabilities.

The foundation of hidden Markov models is a Markov process (chain). It is a stochastic process in which the future distribution of a variable depends only on the variable's current value. Furthermore, this probability does not change over time. To be more formal let us consider a discrete process with N distinct states S, $S = \{S_1, S_2, \ldots, S_N\}$, with q_t denoting a state at time t, so that the observable sequence of states is $q_1q_2q_3 \ldots q_t$. In principle, the probability of transition from the current to the next state would require specification of the current, as well as of all previous states. However, that is not the case with the first order discrete time Markov chains, which have the following properties:

$$a_{ij} = P(q_t = S_j \mid q_{t-1} = S_i, q_{t-2} = S_k, \ldots) = P(q_t = S_j \mid q_{t-1} = S_i) \qquad (1)$$

$$a_{ij} = P(q_t = S_j \mid q_{t-1} = S_i) = P(q_{t+l} = S_j \mid q_{t+l-1} = S_i), \; 1 \le i, j \le N, \forall l \qquad (2)$$

where a_{ij} denotes state transition probabilities (probability that system will make a transition at time t from state S_i to S_j). Equation 1 ensures that the transition probabilities at t+1 depend only on the states at t. Equation 2 guarantees that these probabilities do not change over time (they are the same at time t and $t+1$). The state transition coefficients satisfy standard stochastic constraints given in equation 3.

$$a_{ij} \geq 0, \ \sum_{j=1}^{N} a_{ij} = 1 \tag{3}$$

Note that in the Markov chain the output of the process is the set of states, which is observable. If we extend the model in the way that the observation (some visible symbol emitted in every time step) becomes a probabilistic function of the state, we get a hidden Markov model.

An HMM is a doubly stochastic process with an underlying stochastic process that is hidden, but can be observed through another set of stochastic processes that produce the sequence of observed symbols [13]. A discrete HMM[1] can be formally defined using the following elements:

- T – length of the observation sequence,
- N – the number of states in the model,
- M – the number of distinct observation symbols (the discrete codebook size),
- $S = \{S_1, S_2, \ldots, S_N\}$ – the set of states, with q_t as the state at time t,
- $V = \{v_1, v_2, \ldots, v_M\}$ – the set of observation symbols, with O_t as the observation symbol at time t,
- A – state transition probability distribution, $A = \{a_{ij}\}$, where

$$a_{ij} = P\,(q_t = S_j \mid q_{t-1} = S_i),\ 1 \leq i, j \leq N,$$

- B – observation symbol probability distribution in state j, $B = \{b_j(k)\}$, where

$$b_j(k) = P\,(v_k \ at\ t \mid q_t = S_j)\ ,\ 1 \leq j \leq N,\ 1 \leq k \leq M,$$

- π – initial state distribution, $\pi = \{\ \pi_i\ \}$, where

$$\pi_i = P(q_1 = S_i),\ 1 \leq i \leq N$$

The probability that the observation sequence $O = O_1 O_2 O_3 \ldots O_T$ is generated by the model λ is denoted as $P\,(\,O \mid \lambda\,)$, where each O_t is one of the symbols from V, T is the number of observation in the sequence. The model is defined as $\lambda = (N, M, A, B, \pi)$.

There are three fundamental operations in hidden Markov models:

- The evaluation problem: Given the observation sequence $O = O_1 O_2 O_3 \ldots O_T$ and the model λ, determine the probability $P\,(\,O \mid \lambda\,)$,

[1] Discrete time, but also emits discrete symbols

i.e. the probability that this particular observation sequence was generated by the model λ.

- The learning problem: Given the partial definition of the model λ (the number of states and the number of symbols, but not the state and symbol transition matrices), and a set of training observations, determine probabilities a_{ij}, $b_j(k)$, to maximize $P(O \mid \lambda)$.
- The decoding problem: Given the model λ and the observation sequence $O = O_1O_2O_3...O_T$, determine the most likely sequence of hidden states $Q = q_1q_2q_3...q_T$.

However, a discussion on solutions to these three problems is beyond the scope of this book, and we refer to [13] for a detailed description. Briefly, the forward algorithm is used for the evaluation problem, the Baum-Welch method [14] for training, and the Viterbi algorithm for finding the single best state sequence.

A major development in the theory of hidden Markov models was the maximization technique of Baum et al. [14], which has led to a wide range of theoretical outgrowths. Although continuous [15], and different extensions of discrete HMMs like Pseudo 3-D HMMs [16] are proposed, in most cases first order left-to-right discrete hidden Markov models are used. These models satisfy the following constraints:

$$a_{ij} = 0 \text{ for } j < i,$$
$$\pi_1 = 1.$$

As shown in Figure 5.1, left-to-right models always start from the first state to the left and are allowed to make transitions only toward right states or to the same state.

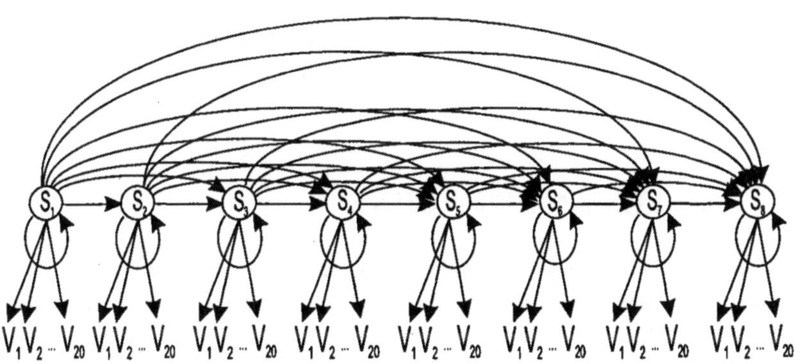

Figure 5.1. An example of a left-to-right hidden Markov model

If the observation sequences are very short, a modified re-estimation formula for the training with multiple observation sequences [17] can be used. Let O^M denote the set of m observation sequences $(O^1, O^2, \ldots, O^m)$, where $O^k = O_1^k O_2^k O_3^k \ldots O_{T_k}^k$ is the kth training sequence with T_k observations, and $\alpha_t(i)$ and $\beta_t(i)$ be forward and backward variables. The forward and backward variables are defined as:

$$\alpha_t(i) = P(O_1 O_2 O_3 \ldots O_T, q_t = S_i \mid \lambda),$$
$$\beta_t(i) = P(O_{t+1} O_{t+2} O_{t+3} \ldots O_T, q_t = S_i \mid \lambda),$$

Then, the re-estimation equation for the transition probability (a_{ij}) can be computed as:

$$a_{ij} = \frac{\sum_k \sum_{t=1}^{T-1} \alpha_t^k(i) a_{ij} b_j(O_{t+1}^k) \beta_{t+1}^k(j)}{\sum_k \sum_{t=1}^{T-1} \alpha_t^k(i) \beta_t^k(j)},$$

while the re-estimation for the probability of observation symbol v_k occurring in state j ($b_j(k)$) is:

$$b_j(k) = \frac{\sum_k \sum_{\substack{t=1 \\ O_t^k = v_k}}^{T-1} \alpha_t^k(i) \beta_1^k(j)}{\sum_k \sum_{t=1}^{T-1} \alpha_t^k(i) \beta_t^k(j)}.$$

In our experiments, we used above equations for computing the transition probability and probability of an observation symbol during the training procedure.

3. BAYESIAN NETWORKS

A Bayesian network is a probabilistic network that has emerged as one of the primary methods for representing and manipulating probabilistic information. Basically, it is a directed acyclic graph that describes dependencies in a probability distribution function defined over a set of variables. The nodes represent variables, while the links between nodes represent the dependencies between the variables. Each variable can assume an arbitrary number of mutually exclusive values.

The Bayesian network can be seen as a representation of a joint probability distribution for all variables. The strength of Bayesian networks is that they have built-in independence assumptions. So, to define the joint probability distribution, one does not need all joint probabilities. For example, the joint distribution of a simple network, given in Figure 5.2, is defined as follows:

$$Pr(a,b,c,d,e,f,g,h) = Pr(a \mid b,c)Pr(b \mid d,e)Pr(c \mid f)Pr(d)Pr(e)Pr(f)$$

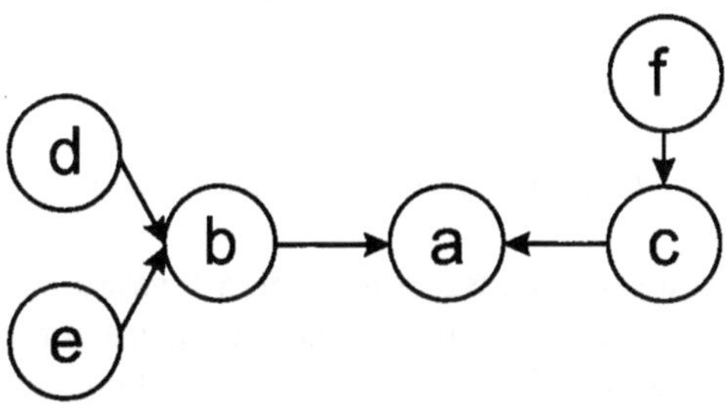

Figure 5.2. A Bayesian network

In order to use a Bayesian network, the network topology, the prior probabilities of all root nodes, and the conditional probabilities are required. Conditional probabilities quantify the effects that parents have on the node. They can be obtained either through the learning process or from expert knowledge. Given these preliminaries, inference can be performed, i.e. the computation of the probability of a subset of variables, having observed the evidence nodes. In other words, whenever a marginal probability is changed, the effects of the observation are propagated throughout the network by efficient algorithms [18] and the other probabilities are updated.

A dynamic Bayesian network is a probabilistic network, which is able to model stochastic temporal processes. It is a special case of singly connected Bayesian networks specifically aimed at time series modeling. A time-slice network is used to represent each snapshot of the evolving temporal process. Therefore, the network grows over time. In DBNs that satisfy the first order Markov property, each state at time *t* may depend on one or more states at time *t-1* and/or some states in the same time instant. The conditional distributions within and between time slices are repeated, so that the network can be specified by only two time slices and links between them (see Figure 5.3). However, when applied, the network grows (unroll) by copying the time-slices and links between them until the appropriate size that accommodates the observation is achieved.

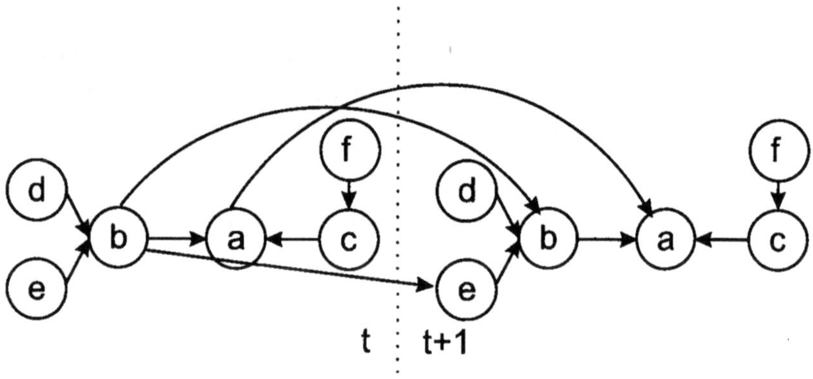

Figure 5.3. A dynamic Bayesian network

As an HMM is a special case of a DBN, a forward-backward algorithm can also be used for computing the probability distributions in DBNs given some known observations. The parameters of a DBN can be learned from a training data set using the Expectation Maximization algorithm. For the description of algorithms for computing with dynamic Bayesian networks, we refer to [19-23].

4. BACK TO THE TENNIS CASE STUDY

As our framework is independent of feature/semantic extractors, it provides users with flexibility of using different pattern recognition techniques for the derivation of semantics from low-level video features. Hence, instead of the grammars, proposed in Chapter 4, we choose here hidden Markov models for event classification, as effective tools for modeling time-varying patterns with automatic learning capabilities.

In the Tennis case study, hidden Markov models are used to recognize different strokes performed by players, such as forehand, backhand, service, etc. The remainder of this section looks back at the video processing and feature extraction process for tennis videos and then describes stroke recognition experiments.

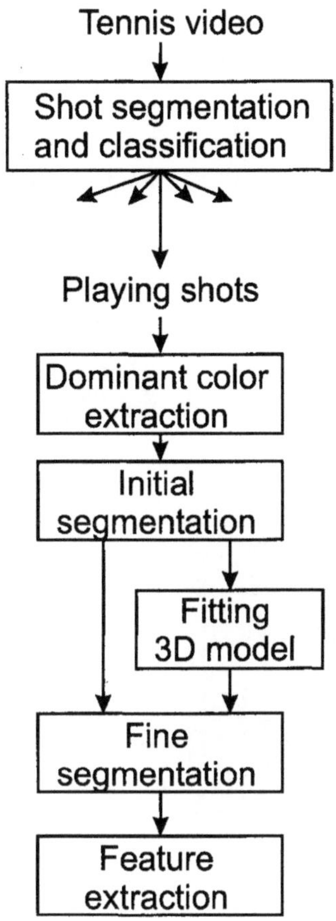

Figure 5.4. Tennis video processing

4.1 Back to tennis video processing

The tennis video processing, which includes segmentation, shot classification, player segmentation, and feature extraction, is described in the previous chapter (sections 3.1 till 3.3). However, the process of player segmentation showed drawbacks when it came to the extraction of some more complex shape features that will be introduced later in this chapter. In order to overcome that problem, we refine the player segmentation algorithm in the next subsection. Using the knowledge about the scene, we develop a robust scheme for image segmentation that gradually leads us to the solution. Figure 5.4 surveys the whole process of visual analysis that includes two new steps: fitting the 3D model and fine segmentation. In the sequel, we briefly describe the player segmentation and feature extraction. A more detailed description is given in [24].

Figure 5.5. Player segmentation: (a) Original image; (b) Initial segmentation; (c) 3D model after fitting to the lines; (d) Final segmentation.

4.2 Player segmentation

The segmentation algorithm is divided into three steps:

Step1: Using estimated statistics of the tennis field color (see [24] for details), we perform the initial quadratic segmentation of the image, as shown in Figure 5.5b. The player is detected as the largest compact region in the lower half of the image by applying morphological operations, such as erosion and dilation.

Step 2: After thinning, the initial segmentation is used to fit the tennis court model. The model is fitted by applying the Gauss-Newton minimization procedure on Gaussian blurred images. Multiple starting points are used for the initial sequence images together with the multi-scale approach using Gaussian pyramid [25] to increase the convergence area. The 3D model is constructed having in mind the visibility of the lines.

Step 3: After fitting the 3D model, we get more knowledge about the scene at a higher semantic level (Figure 5.5c). This knowledge together with the initially segmented player is used to form the start values for the robust estimation of the parameters of a number of Gaussian models. Model parameters for the colors of the field, the lines, and eventually the net are estimated using the data from some neighborhood of the initially detected player. These values are then used to refine the player segmentation.

We do not expect the player to have the same color as the field or the net. On the other hand, the players often have white clothes similar to the color of the field lines. Distinction here is done using our knowledge about the line positions. We discard all the structures that are thin in the line direction and are positioned according to the fitted model. Unfortunately, this can result in removing isolated thin white color parts of the player, when they are aligned and overlapped with the field lines. Luckily, these situations are very rare.

4.3 Feature extraction

This section describes extraction of features, characterizing the shape of the newly segmented player's binary representation. Having the specific case of the human figure in this particular application, we extract special parameters trying to maximize their informativeness. Famous Johansson's moving light displays [26] and some recent results in recognizing human activities from their binary representations [27, 28] motivated our approach. Besides the features already mentioned in Chapter 3 and Chapter 4, we extract the following specific features:

- The position of the upper half of the silhouette with respect to the mass center ($f_{10\text{-}11}$), its orientation (f_{12}), and the eccentricity (f_{13}). Those features describe the upper part of the body that contains most of the information.
- For each circle cutout that is centered at the mass center, we count the percentage of pixels in the pie ($f_{14\text{-}21}$) as shown in Figure 5.6b. This can be seen as a general approximate description.

The sticking-out parts ($f_{22\text{-}23}$) are extracted similar to [27] by filtering and finding local maximums of the distance from a point at the contour to the mass center. Only certain angles are considered, as indicated in Figure 5.6c.

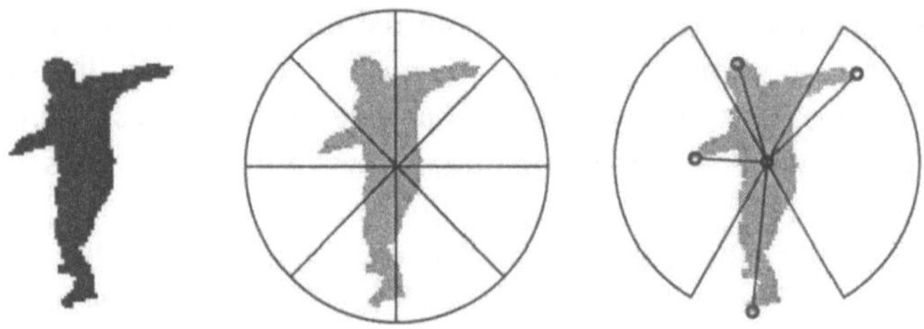

(a) (b) (c)

Figure 5.6. Specific features: (a) extracted shape; (b) pie features; (c) skeleton features.

The following table lists all extracted features.

Table 5.1. Features extracted from tennis videos

f_1	Color histogram
f_2	Dominant color
$f_{3\text{-}4}$	Entropy characteristics
f_5	Skin colored pixels
f_6	Player position
f_7	Area
f_8	Orientation
f_9	Eccentricity
$f_{10\text{-}11}$	Mass centre of the upper half
f_{12}	Orientation of the upper half
f_{13}	Eccentricity of the upper half
$f_{14\text{-}21}$	Pie features
$f_{22\text{-}23}$	Skeleton features

4.4 Stroke recognition

Having the features extracted, we conduct series of stroke recognition experiments to demonstrate the validity of our approach. The experiments, we carry out, are divided into two series, based on different stroke classification used. For the recognition of different strokes based on a set of extracted features, we use hidden Markov models and exploit their automatic learning capabilities.

In our experiments, we use ordinary TV broadcast tennis videos with different players at different tournaments: Australian Open (Sampras, Agassi, Hingis, V. Williams, S. Williams, Kournikova, Davenport, etc.), Swisscom Challenge, Vienna Open, etc.

For stroke recognition, we use first order, left-to-right, discrete hidden Markov models. Discrete HMMs require translation of continuous feature parameters (listed in Table 5.1) into symbols from a predefined set (codebook). In contrast to independent quantization of each feature parameter, we perform here the joint quantization of a group of feature parameters, which is termed vector quantization. The vector quantization process reduces the data redundancy, but introduces distortion between feature parameters and the data represented by a codebook. In order to perform quantization, first the codebook is generated. In this process *n*-dimensional space is partitioned into M clusters, where *n* is the number of feature parameters in our case, while M is the codebook size. A simple example of a quantization process, where two feature parameters are jointly quantized using a codebook size of three symbols (A, B, C), is given in Figure 5.7. Quantization implies that any feature vector is represented by one of the three symbols. For example, the feature vector {100, 100} is represented by symbol B. After the design of the codebook, each observation (feature vector) is classified as one of the symbols from the codebook.

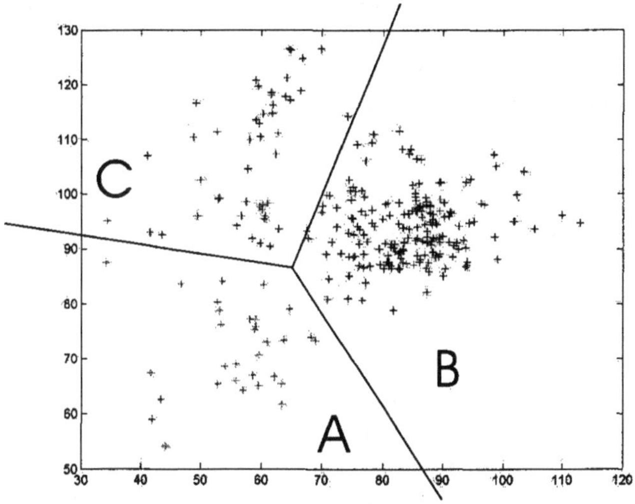

Figure 5.7. Feature quantization

In order to design a codebook, we use an iterative clustering algorithm known in the pattern-recognition literature as the k-means algorithm [29]. However, the k-means algorithm can only converge to a local minimum of the quantization error. Hence, we repeat it a number of times with different initial values for cluster centres, and then choose the clustering with the minimum overall quantization error. Selection of the codebook size is a trade-off between a smaller quantization error (larger codebook size) and faster HMM operations (smaller codebook size). We try various codebook sizes in the range of 8-80 symbols.

Prior to stroke recognition, we have to perform the learning procedures, and train the adequate number of HMMs to recognize specific classes of strokes. Training sequences are manually selected, using a tool that is developed for video annotation and pre-processing. The selected sequences are classified according to used classification, which differs in the two series of experiments.

We set up the HMM parameters, which include the number of states and the size of a codebook, based on some heuristics. After trying different codebook sizes and number of states from 4 to 48, we select the codebook size of 24 symbols and HMMs with 8 states.

In the learning process, we train 50 different models for each stroke class using the Baum-Welch algorithm with the modified re-estimation formula for the training with multiple observation sequences (see Section 1). Different initial parameters are used for each model. As a final result, we select the model with the highest probability to represent a class of strokes. Having the models for each class of strokes, we perform stroke recognition using the first order, left-to-right, discrete HMMs.

4.4.1 Experiment 1

In the first experiment, we aim at achieving two goals: (1) to determine the best feature set and (2) to investigate person independence of different feature sets. Hence, we perform a number of experiments with different feature combinations. In order to examine how invariant they are on different players including female ones, two series of experiments are conducted: $1a$ and $1b$. In the series $1a$, we use the same player in the training and evaluation sets, while in $1b$ HMMs are trained with one group of players, but strokes performed by another group are evaluated. In both cases, the training set contains 120 different video sequences, while the evaluation set contains 240 sequences (each sequence corresponds to one stroke).

To be able to roughly compare our results with [2], we select the same six events to be recognized: forehand, backhand, service, smash, forehand volley, and backhand volley. In each experiment, six hidden Markov models are constructed - one for each type of events we would like to recognize. Each stroke sequence is evaluated by all six hidden Markov models (parallel evaluation). The one with the highest probability is selected as the result.

The recognition accuracies in Table 5.2 (percentages of rightly classified strokes using parallel evaluation) show that the combination of pie and skeleton features ($f_{14\text{-}23}$) achieves the highest accuracy in the experiment $1a$. The recognition rates drop in experiment $1b$ as expected. Two feature combinations show to be the most person independent, i.e. invariant on different player constitutions. The first is the combination of eccentricity, the mass center of the upper part, and skeleton features, while another is the combination of orientation, eccentricity, and skeleton features. The optimal result with this combination of features is achieved with the codebook size of 24 symbols and HMMs with 8 states.

Table 5.2. Recognition results (%)

Feat.\Ex.	1*a*	1*b*	2
$f_{8\text{-}11}$	82	79	76
$f_{8\text{-}13}$	85	82	80
$f_{8\text{-}9,\,12\text{-}13}$	81	78	76
$f_{8\text{-}9,\,22\text{-}23}$	89	88	87
$f_{8\text{-}23}$	86	82	79
$f_{9\text{-}11,\,22\text{-}23}$	91	89	88
$f_{14\text{-}21}$	85	78	78
$f_{14\text{-}23}$	93	87	86

4.4.2 Experiment 2

In the second experiment, we investigate recognition rates of different feature combinations using an extensive classification of strokes from the tennis literature [30]. There are 11 different strokes: service, backhand slice, backhand spin, backhand spin two-handed, forehand slice, forehand spin, smash, forehand volley, forehand half-volley, backhand volley, and backhand half-volley. The training set and the evaluation set remain the same as in experiment 1*b*, only the new classification is applied.

Although at first glance some strokes in this new classification are very similar to each other (for example volley and half-volley or backhand slice and spin), the performance (Table 5.2, last column) drops only slightly. The results prove that there is an evident difference between backhand slice and spin stroke for example. The arm position and the swing are different. In this experiment, the majority of false recognitions remain the same as in experiment 1. Nearly 65% comes from forehands recognized as backhands and vice versa, as well as from forehand-volleys recognized as forehands and vice versa. A reason for that can also be an unbalanced number of strokes in different stroke classes in the test set. For example, the number of forehand slice and forehand half-valley strokes was much smaller than the number of services, backhand slice, and backhand spin strokes. A bigger test collection with the exactly same number of strokes in each stroke groups would lead to a more comprehensive analysis of misrecognition in this experiment with the expanded classification of tennis strokes.

4.4.3 Discussion

In experiment 1*b*, we have achieved the recognition accuracy that is for about 20% higher than the corresponding accuracy reported in [2]. We believe that the enhancement is due to a more efficient training algorithm and mostly from improved, more informative, and invariant features (in the first place novel skeleton features). The improvement we achieved is certainly more significant taking into account that we used TV video scenes with a very small player's shape compared to the close-ups used in [2]. However, the smaller player's shape and our choice for more invariant features have resulted in the slightly poorer accuracy of our system compared to [2] in experiment 1*a*. Note that the conclusions about the reasons for different performance are intuitive. For a rigorous comparison, the same feature and data sets and the same training algorithm should have been used.

In order to improve the performance of our approach, one could further fine-tune feature extraction taking into consideration human body parts and their kinematics. The use of shape axis model introduced by Liu and Geiger [31] would be interesting in this context. On the other hand, having the ball position known (an attempt is reported in [32]) would certainly make the distinction between forehands and backhands as well as between volleys and half-valleys more robust and significantly increase the recognition rate.

The approach presented here has some limitations. The performance of stroke recognition depends on the camera position and the noise strength, as skeleton features are very sensitive on video quality. Some features are also dependent on the resolution of input images. Furthermore, we used only right-handed players in our experiments. Introducing left-handed player would require training of additional HMMs and further experiments to assess the accuracy of stroke recognition of mixed right- and left-handed players. However, an easier way is to use conceptual information from the player profile and then choose the right HMMs for recognition.

Finally, let us look at performance with respect to time required for computation. The segmentation algorithm takes approximately 5.5 minutes per stroke, containing 45 frames (initial segmentation 95s, fitting the 3D model 150s, final segmentation 105s, and feature extraction 40s) on a dual-Pentium II on 350MHz.

The training procedure for a model with 20 different sequences (each approximately 45 frames), which is conducted by doing 50 iterations of the Baum-Welch algorithm with the modified re-estimation formula for the training with multiple observation sequences, takes from 12 seconds for a model with 4 states and 8-symbol codebook size to approximately 20 minutes for a model with 48 states and 80 symbols.

5. FORMULA 1 CASE STUDY

The aim of the Formula 1 case study is twofold. Firstly, we investigate the effectiveness of Bayesian and dynamic Bayesian networks for content-based video retrieval. Secondly, we analyze the applicability of these networks for the fusion of multimodalities in the retrieval process. In particular, we center our attention on fusing the evidence obtained from different media information sources in order to derive the video content. The approach is validated in the particular domain of Formula 1 race videos. For that specific domain, we introduce a robust audio-visual feature extraction scheme, as well as a text recognition and detection method. Based on numerous experiments performed for fusing extracted features in order to extract highlights, we give some recommendations with respect to the modeling of temporal and atemporal dependences in Bayesian networks. A detailed description of the Formula 1 case study can be found in [33].

The remainder of this section is organized as follows. Section 5.1 describes three different media components of TV broadcasting Formula 1 programs: audio, video, and text. The next three sections describe the extraction of multi-modal cues obtained from the three information sources. Section 5.5 illustrates the data set used for evaluation and lists the extracted features. In Section 5.6, we focus on the extraction of excited speech from Formula 1 videos, as the main indication that leads us to highlights. This section also describes several experiments done to investigate properties of dynamic Bayesian networks, as well as to validate our approach. To improve the recall of the recognized highlights based on audio features only, we integrate visual features in the network. This fusion of multi-modal features using dynamic Bayesian networks, aiming at characterizing the highlights of Formula 1 races, is presented in Section 5.7.

5.1 Information sources

As the majority of techniques for event detection, which rely solely on the one-media cues, showed to have robustness problems, we base our analysis on the fusion of the evidence obtained from different information sources. In particular, we concentrate on three different media: audio, video, and text.

Audio plays a significant role in the detection and recognition of events in video. In our domain, the importance of the audio signal is even bigger, since it encapsulates the reporter's comment, which can be considered as a kind of the on-line human annotation of a Formula 1 race. Generally, audio information is highly correlated with visual information. Furthermore, the occurrence of important events that can be classified as highlights is most of the time characterized by the commentator very well. Whenever something important happens the announcer raises his voice due to his excitement, which is a good indication for the highlights.

Visual information has been widely used for video characterization. It yields large and significant information about the video content, but consequently it is the most difficult one to automatically understand. Furthermore, the processing of visual information is very time consuming. Therefore, with regard to visual features, we choose for a trade-off between the effectiveness of the video cues and the cost of their computation.

The third information source we use is the text that is superimposed on the screen. This is another type of on-line annotation done by the TV program producer, which is intended to help viewers to better understand the video content. The superimposed text often brings some additional information that is difficult or even impossible to deduce solely by looking at the video signal. As examples in the Formula 1 program, think of the fastest speed, lap time, order, or the visual difference between the two Ferrari cars of Michael Schumacher and Rubens Barrichello, which are almost the same[2] and can be distinguished only by diverse drivers' helmets.

5.2 Audio characterization

The audio signal of TV Formula 1 programs is very complex and ambiguous. It consists of human speech, car noise, and various background noises, such as cheering, horns, etc. Usually, the Formula 1 program involves two or more announcers, pit reports, and on-line reports given by the Formula 1 drivers. Car noise includes roaring of F1 engines, or the car braking noise. Extraction of basic characteristics from these audio recordings, which consist of complex mixtures of frequencies, is a demanding and challenging task.

Despite this, we use the audio signal to find the segments with announcer's exited speech, as well as the segments in which specific keywords are mentioned.

5.2.1 Audio features used

Based on a few experiments, we make a selection among the variety of features that can be extracted from the audio signal. We choose Short Time Energy (STE), pitch, Mel-Frequency Cepstral Coefficients (MFCCs), and pause rate.

[2] In the season 2001, the only difference between the cars was the very small yellow mark on the camera of Barrichello's car

Short time energy represents average waveform amplitude, defined over a specific time window. We employ Hamming window filter for the calculation of STE, because it brings the best results for speech endpoint detection. STE is usually computed after performing sub-band division of the wide range signal. Indicative bands for speech characterization are lower sub-bands.

Pitch is the fundamental frequency of an audio signal. In general, only speech and harmonic music have well-defined pitch, but still it can be used to characterize any audio form. Among many techniques that have been proposed for pitch estimation and tracking [34], we use the autocorrelation analysis. All techniques for pitch estimation demand the appropriate bandwidth of audio signal for an accurate estimation of pitch. Since human speech is usually under 1 kHz, we are particularly interested in determining pitch that is under this frequency range.

Mel-Frequency Cepstral Coefficients are widely used for speech recognition [35]. They are based on Mel-scale. Mel-scale is gradually warped linear spectrum, with coarser resolution on higher, and finer resolution on lower frequencies. It is metrically adapted to the human perception system. Based on this division, the Mel-frequency sub-band energy is defined. MFCCs are a simple cosine transform of the Mel-scale energy for different filtered sub-bands.

The pause rate feature is intended to determine the quantity of speech in an audio clip. It can be used as an indication of the emphasized human speech. We calculate it by counting the number of silent audio frames in an audio clip.

5.2.2 Audio analysis

To be able to classify human speech as excited, first the speech endpoint detection has to be performed. To end this, we employ short time energy for filtered audio signal and MFCCs. We use 0-882Hz filtered audio signal in the calculation of short time energy, because this bandwidth diminishes car noises and various background noises as well. Only the first three coefficients of the total number of 12 Mel-Frequency Cepstral Coefficients are used in our analysis, because they are shown to be most indicative for speech detection. We calculate the values of these two features for each audio frame, their average values and dynamic range, and maximum values of STE for audio clips. After setting the appropriate thresholds for these parameters, we perform speech endpoint analysis of the audio signal. The thresholds, we use, are 2.2×10^{-3} for the weighted sum of the average and maximum values, and dynamic range of STE, and 1.3 for the sum of the average values and dynamic range of the first three Mel-frequency cepstral coefficients. As a result, we get an indication for each audio clip (0.1s segment) whether it can be considered as a speech or non-speech segment. For the speech endpoint detection, we have also performed some experiments with the entropy and zero crossing rate features, but they showed powerless when applied in a noisy environment such as ours.

For the detection of emphasized speech, we use STE, MFCCs, pitch, and pause rate. Different frequency bands are used for different features. For STE, we use filtered audio signal, 882Hz - 2205Hz, while for MFCCs and pitch we use low passed audio signal, 0 - 882Hz. We compute average and maximum values in an audio clip for all these features obtained for audio frames. Additionally, we compute dynamic range for STE and pitch. These computations are only performed on speech segments, which are obtained by the speech endpoint detection algorithm. Such calculated features are then used by a probabilistic system to detect excited speech.

For the recognition of specific keywords, a keyword-spotting tool, which is based on a finite state grammar [36], is used. We extract a couple of tens of words that can be usually heard when the commentator is excited or when it is a specific part of the race that we are interested in. Two different acoustic models are tried for this purpose. One is trained for clean speech, while the other is aimed at word recognition in TV news. The latter shows better results and as such it is employed in our system. Keyword spotting results in a considerably high accuracy, but note that even better results could be obtained using an acoustic model created especially for the Formula 1 TV program.

The keyword spotting system calculates the non-normalized probability for each word that is specified, the starting time when the word is recognized, as well as the duration of the recognized word. After normalization, the parameters obtained from the audio analysis are used as inputs of a probabilistic network that detects excited speech.

5.3 Visual characterization

In the pre-processing step of our visual analysis, we segment a race video into shots. As in the Tennis case study, we calculate the histogram difference among several consecutive frames. This algorithm results in the accuracy of over 90%, which we consider satisfying.

The visual analysis aims at the extraction of the visual indications that can be used to characterize replay scenes, as well as three different events, namely the start of a race, passing, and fly-out events.

The Formula 1 program usually contains a number of replay scenes. They are very important, since they always contain interesting events. The replay scenes in the Formula 1 program are usually neither slowed down nor marked. They start and finish with special shot change operations termed Digital Video Effects (DVEs). The problem is that these DVEs vary very often, even in the same race and consequently must be frequently learned. Therefore, we employ a more general algorithm based on motion flow and pattern matching [33].

Finally, we extract some visual features that indicate the three events we want to find: start, passing, and fly-out. Start is defined by two parameters: (1) the amount of motion in the scene, and (2) the semaphore presence in the image. To detect the amount of motion, we use pixel color difference between two consecutive frames. The semaphore is described as a rectangular shape, because the distance between red circles is small and they touch each other (Figure 5.8). This rectangular shape is increasing its horizontal dimension in regular time intervals, i.e. after a constant number of video frames (as a new red light is turned on). The rectangular region is detected by filtering the red component of the RGB color representation of a still image.

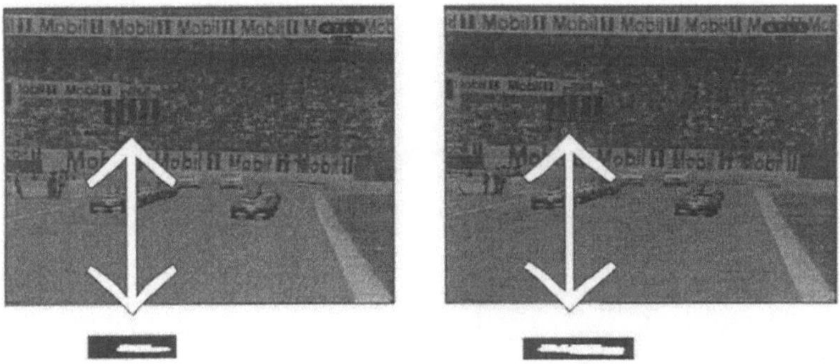

Figure 5.8. Semaphore with three and four lights on

For passing, we calculate the changes of the number of pixels that have the color of the race track in several consecutive pictures. This is used to compute the probability that there is a chance of one car passing another. Note that we employ very general visual feature for the passing detection. By applying more powerful techniques for object detection and tracking, we could obtain much more specific features that would lead to better results.

Fly outs usually come with a lot of sand and dust. Therefore, we recognize presence of these two characteristics in the picture. We filter the RGB image for these colors and compute the probability that will be later used by a probabilistic network.

5.4 Text detection and recognition

The text that appears in a digital video can be broadly divided into two classes: scene text and graphic text. The scene text occurs as a natural part of the actual scene, which is captured by the camera. Examples in our domain include billboards, text on vehicles, writings on human clothes, etc. The graphic (superimposed) text, which is the point of our interest, is mechanically added text to video frames in order to supplement the visual and audio content. It usually brings much more useful information, since it represents additional information for better understanding of a video scene, and is closely related to it.

Since the process of text detection and recognition is complex, we will divide it into three steps, as follows: (1) text detection, (2) refinement of text regions, and (3) text recognition. An example of text detection and recognition is shown in Figure 5.9.

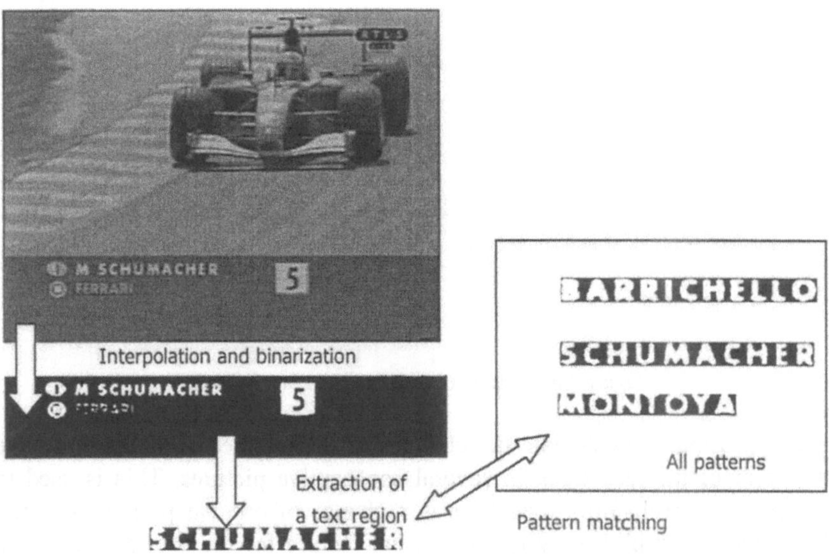

Since the number of frames in a typical Formula 1 video is large, processing each frame for text recognition is not computationally feasible. Therefore, the first step of the text recognition task will be to find frames with text regions. Here, we use the property of the Formula 1 domain that the superimposed text is placed in the bottom part of the image, while the background is shaded in order to make characters clearer, sharpened, and easier to read. The characters are usually drawn with high contrast to the shaded background. The tree different colors of characters are used: light blue, yellow, and white. To detect whether the superimposed text is present in an image, we simply need to process the bottom part of the image.

The algorithm we use is a two-pass text detection algorithm. In the first pass, the algorithm analyzes if the shaded region is present in each frame of a video sequence. By counting the number of the shaded regions in consecutive frames, we skip all the short segments that do not satisfy the duration criteria. In the second pass, we calculate the duration, number, and variance of bright pixels present in these shaded regions. If computed values satisfy constraints defined for the text detection algorithm, then this video sequence is marked as a segment that contains the superimposed text.

Such segments are further processed in the refinement process, which consists of next steps: (1) filtering of text regions and (2) interpolation of text regions. The text regions have to be filtered in order to enable better separation from the background, as well as for sharpening the edges of characters. The filtering is done through minimizing or maximizing pixel intensities over several consecutive frames. However, this filtering is not sufficient for text recognition. Therefore, we employ an interpolation algorithm to enlarge characters and make them clearer and cleaner. The interpolation algorithm magnifies the text area four times in both directions. After this refinement, the text regions have much better character representations and they are ready for the text recognition step.

The algorithm for text recognition is based on pattern matching techniques, mainly because of the uniform structure and a small number of different words superimposed on the screen. These words are names of the Formula 1 drivers and some informative words, such as pit stop, final lap, classification, winner, etc. Since the processing of a color image is computationally expensive and slow, we extract reference patterns and perform matching with black-white images. The black-white text regions are obtained from the color text regions by filtering RGB components. After applying thresholds to the text region, we mark characters as white regions on the black background. For character extraction, the horizontal and the vertical projection of white pixels are used. Since characters can have different heights, we use a double vertical projection in order to refine the characters better. However, we do not match characters to reference character patterns because they are usually irregular and can be occluded or deformed. Thus, we connect characters that belong to one word into a region. This is done based on the pixel distance between characters. Regions that are close to each other are considered as characters that belong to the same word.

Having the regions containing one word extracted, we perform pattern matching. To speed up the matching algorithm, we separate the patterns of words into several categories based on their length. The matching procedure is performed only for reference patterns with a similar length. A simple metric of pixel difference is used for pattern matching. By specifying an appropriate threshold, we are able to recognize the superimposed words. Thus, a reference pattern with the largest metric above this threshold is selected as a matched word. A more detailed description of the text detection and recognition algorithm is given in [33].

The above described algorithm gives a higher recognition accuracy than an algorithm that recognize separate characters. However, this is achieved at the cost of flexibility. Our approach cannot recognize the text which reference pattern is not in the database (for example the name of a new driver). Therefore, it requires regular updates of these patterns. Luckily, the introduction of new drivers, fonts, and words superimposed in the broadcast of Formula 1 races is rare and usually happens at the beginning of a new season.

5.5 Data set and audio-visual features

We digitize three Formula 1 races of the 2001 season, namely, the German, Belgian, and USA Grand Prix. The average duration of a Formula 1 race is about 90 minutes or 135,000 frames for a PAL video. Videos are digitized as a quarter of the PAL standard resolution (384x288). Audio is sampled at 22 kHz with 16 bits per audio sample.

Feature values, which are extracted from the audio and video signal, are represented as probabilistic values in the range from zero to one. Since the parameters are calculated for each 0.1s, the length of feature vectors is ten times longer than the duration of the video measured in seconds. The features we extracted from a Formula 1 video are: keywords (f_1), pause rate (f_2), average values of short time energy (f_3), dynamic range of short time energy (f_4), maximum values of short time energy (f_5), average values of pitch (f_6), dynamic range of pitch (f_7), maximum values of pitch (f_8), average values of MFCCs (f_9), maximum values of MFCCs (f_{10}), part of the race (f_{11}), replay (f_{12}), color difference (f_{13}), semaphore (f_{14}), dust (f_{15}), sand (f_{16}), and the difference of racetrack-colored pixels (f_{17}). Since we also employ text detection and recognition algorithms, we are also able to extract text from the video. We extract the names of Formula 1 drivers and the semantic content of superimposed text (for example, if it is a pit stop or driver's classification is shown, etc.).

5.6 Excited speech

This subsection demonstrates how dynamic Bayesian networks can be effectively used for the extraction of excited speech based on the evidence obtained from the described audio analysis. We perform numerous experiments to compare Bayesian Networks (BNs) versus Dynamic Bayesian Networks (DBNs), different network structures, temporal dependences, and learning algorithms.

As we work with DBNs that have hidden states, we employ the Expectation Maximization algorithm for the BN/DBN learning. For inference, the modified Boyen-Koller algorithm for approximate inference is used. A detailed description of these algorithms can be found in [33].

The main goal of the experiments is to automatically determine the segments of the audio signal that contain excited speech. In addition, we compare the results that can be achieved by employing BNs versus DBNs, using different network structures. Therefore, we develop three different structures of BNs for processing only audio cues, and corresponding DBN structures for the same purpose. The intention is to explore how different network structures can influence the inference step in this type of networks. The structures of BNs, which are also used for one time slice of DBNs, are depicted in Figure 5.10.

The query node is Excited Announcer (EA), since we want to determine whether the announcer raises his voice due to an interesting event that was taking place in the race. The shaded nodes represent evidence nodes, which receive their values based on features extracted from the audio signal of the Formula 1 video.

The temporal dependencies between nodes from two consecutive time slices of DBNs are defined as in Figure 5.11. With respect to learning and inference algorithms, we consider all the nodes from one time slice as belonging to the same cluster.

We learn the BN and DBN parameters on a sequence of 300s, consisting of 3000 evidence values, extracted from the audio signal. The video sequence consists of 12 segments with 25s duration each. The inference is performed on audio evidence extracted from the whole digitized German Grand Prix. For each network structure, we compute precision and recall.

Note that we have to process the results obtained from BNs since the output values cannot be directly employed to distinguish the presence and time boundaries of the excited speech. This is shown in Figure 5.12a. Therefore, we accumulate the values of a query node over time to make a conclusion whether the announcer is excited.

The results obtained from a dynamic Bayesian network are much smoother (see Figure 5.12b), and we do not have to process the output. We just employ a threshold to decide whether the announcer is excited.

The results from conducted experiments with previously described networks are shown in Table 5.3.

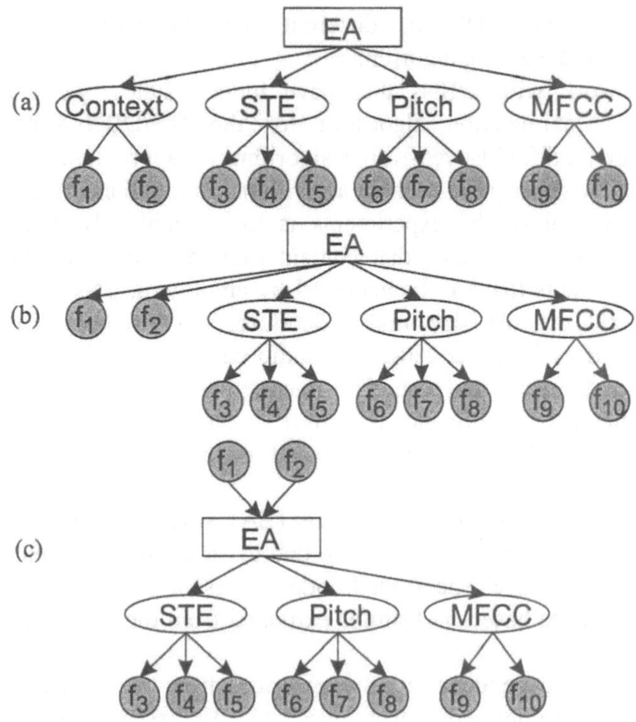

Figure 5.10. Different structures for processing of audio features: a) Fully parameterized structure; b) Structure with direct influence from the evidence to query nodes; c) Input/output BN structure

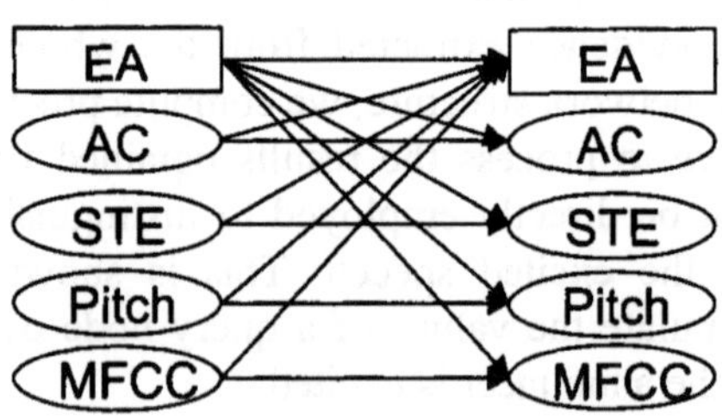

Figure 5.11. Temporal dependencies of the dynamic Bayesian networks

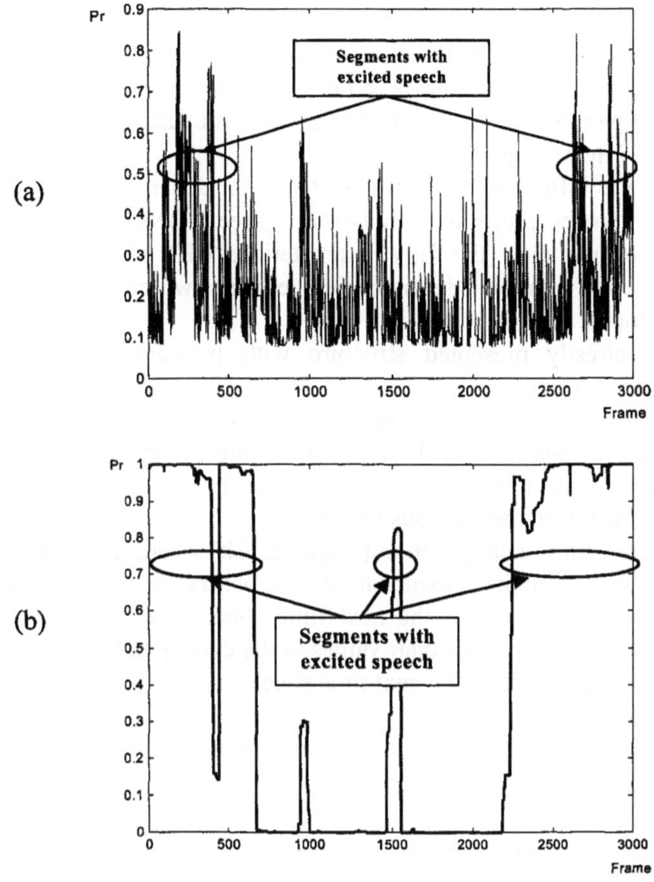

Figure 5.12. Inference results for 300s long video sequence with a) an audio BN; and b) an audio DBN

Table 5.3. Comparison of BNs and DBNs for the detection of emphasized speech

Network structure	BN (Fig. 5.10a)	BN (Fig. 5.10b)	BN (Fig. 5.10c)	DBN (Fig. 5.10a, Fig. 5.11)
Precision	61 %	54 %	50 %	85 %
Recall	67 %	62 %	76 %	81 %

By comparing different BN structures, we can see that there is no significant difference in precision and recall obtained from them. The corresponding DBNs perform similarly except for the DBN that corresponds to the BN with fully parameterized structure (Figure 5.10a). It gives much better results than other BN/DBN networks (last column in Table 5.3). To see whether those results are the best ones that we can obtain from the extracted audio parameters, we conduct more experiments with DBNs that will be described in the sequel.

We explore the influence that different temporal dependencies have on learning and inference procedures in DBNs. Three DBNs with the same structure of one time slice (the fully parameterized DBN shown in Figure 5.10a), but different temporal dependencies between two consecutive time slices are developed:

- The already presented structure with temporal dependencies shown in Figure 5.11.
- A DBN with an 'emission' temporal structure (Figure 5.13a), where all non-observable nodes distribute evidence to the query nodes in the next time slice and only the query node receives evidence from the previous time slice.
- A 'collecting' configuration (Figure 5.13b) where the query node does not distribute evidence to all non-observable nodes, but only to the query node of the next time slice. Here, all other non-observable nodes pass their values to the corresponding nodes and to the query node of the next time slice.

The evaluation shows that the first structure significantly outperforms the second and slightly the third one.

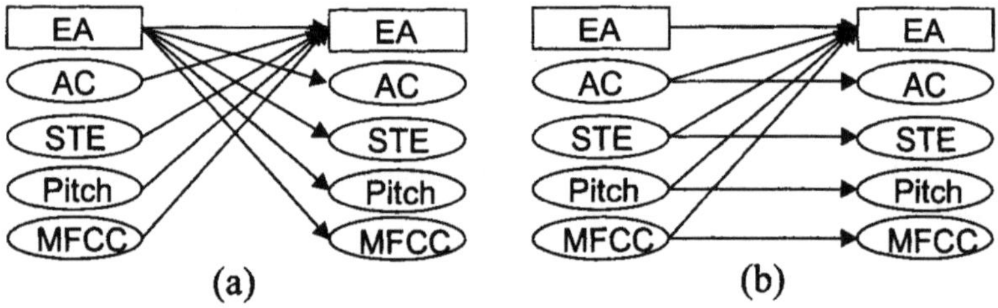

Figure 5.13. Different temporal dependencies: a) emission, b) collecting

In addition, we perform experiments with different clusters formed in the fully parameterized DBN structure. Since our network is relatively simple, we conduct only one experiment with clustering. In this experiment, we separate non-observable nodes from the other part of the network, as proposed by Boyen and Coller in [37]. In the original network, all the nodes from one time slice are assumed to be in the same cluster. The evaluation shows that the clustering technique does not bring significant changes of the recall parameter, but results in a larger number of misclassified sequences.

Conclusions from the experiments performed are twofold. From the first group of experiments, we conclude that the DBN learning and inference procedures depend a lot on the selected DBN structure for one time slice. We can see that this is not the case when inference and learning are performed with BNs. The experiments have shown the advantages of the fully parameterized DBN structure over the other BN/DBN networks. Secondly, we conclude that chosen temporal dependencies between nodes of two consecutive time slices have strong influence on the results of DBN inference. The best result has been obtained with the fully parameterized DBN structure with temporal dependencies depicted in Figure 5.11. To evaluate the selected network structure, we employ it for the detection of the emphasized speech in the audio signal of all three races (Table 5.4).

Table 5.4. Extraction of excited speech with the audio DBN

Race	German GP	Belgian GP	USA GP
Precision	85 %	77 %	76 %
Recall	81 %	79 %	81 %

5.7 Highlights

The audio DBN can only extract the segments of the Formula 1 race where the announcer raises his voice. Other interesting segments (highlights), which are missed by the announcer, could not be extracted. Therefore, the employment of the audio DBN for highlight extraction would lead to high precision, but low recall (if we count replay scenes, recall is about 50%).

To improve the results obtained solely from audio indications, we develop an audio-visual DBN for highlight detection. The structure that represents one time slice of this network is depicted in Figure 5.14. The Highlight node is chosen to be the main query node, while we also query nodes: Start, Fly Out, and Passing, in our experiments. Chosen temporal dependencies among nodes in this network are shown in Figure 5.15.

Experiments are done similarly as for the audio BN/DBNs. We employ the learning algorithm on 6 sequences with 50s duration each. The results obtained by applying the audio-visual DBN to the German Grand Prix are shown in Table 5.5. Precision and recall for highlights are calculated based on the probability threshold of 0.5 and minimal time duration of 6s (the segments shorter than 6 seconds are ignored).

The values of the other query nodes are calculated based on the value of the main query node (highlight). We calculate most probable candidates during each "highlight" segment, and pronounce it as a start, fly out, or passing based on values of corresponding nodes. For segments longer than 15s, we perform this operation every 5s to enable multiple selections.

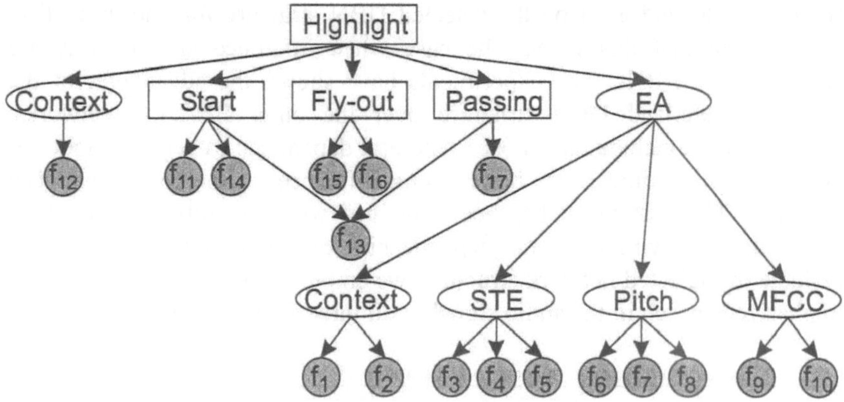

Figure 5.14. Audio-visual DBN for one time slice

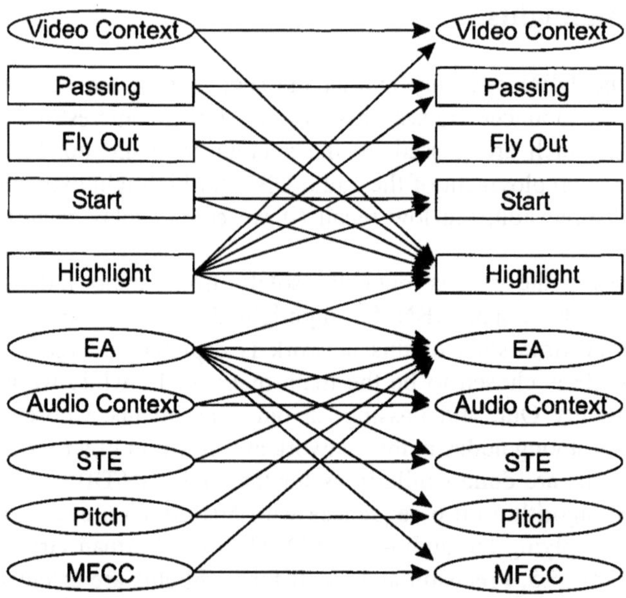

Figure 5.15. Temporal dependencies of the audio-visual DBN

The supplemental query nodes are incorporated in the scheme in order to classify different interesting events that take place in the Formula 1 race. For the German Grand Prix (Table 5.5), we gain high accuracy for highlights and start, while most misclassifications are for fly out and passing events. Main reason for this is that we use very general video cues that do not characterize very well the fly out event, as well as the passing event.

Table 5.5. Evaluation results of the audio-visual DBN applied to German GP

Event/Race		German Grand Prix
Highlights	Precision	84 %
	Recall	86 %
Start	Precision	83 %
	Recall	100 %
Fly Out	Precision	64 %
	Recall	78 %
Passing	Precision	79 %
	Recall	50 %

For the Belgium and the USA Grand Prix, we have a big decrement in our results, mostly because of the "passing" part of the network. Therefore, we simplify the overall audio-visual network, and exclude the "passing" sub-network. A significant difference in results obtained with (Belgian Grand Prix) and without the passing sub-network (USA Grand Prix) is presented in Table 5.6. The network with the passing sub-network performs fine in the case of the German Grand Prix, but fails with the other two races. The explanation for this is a different camera work in the German Grand Prix. This emphasizes the importance of data representation and confirms the fact that general low-level visual features might yield very poor results in the context of high-level concepts. Obviously, more domain dependent features, which characterize the trajectories of Formula 1 cars, will be much robust and give a better result for the passing event.

Table 5.6. Evaluation results for the audio-visual DBN

Event/Race		Belgian Grand Prix[3]	USA Grand Prix
Highlights	Precision	43 %	73 %
	Recall	53 %	76 %
Start	Precision	100 %	100 %
	Recall	67 %	50 %
Fly Out	Precision	100 %	NA[4]
	Recall	36 %	NA
Passing	Precision	28 %	
	Recall	31 %	

[3] These results are obtained by the DBN that includes the passing sub-network

[4] There were no fly-outs in the USA Grand Prix

6. SUMMARY

This chapter has focused on stochastic techniques for video modeling, and demonstrated how they could be successfully used for content-based video retrieval. In particular, we have centered our attention on hidden Markov models and Bayesian networks.

The selection of hidden Markov models was motivated by their success in a range of applications that involved time-sequential data, particularly in speech recognition, but also recently in gesture and handwriting recognition. In this chapter, HMMs have been applied for the characterization of tennis videos, i.e. for the recognition of different tennis strokes. Consequently, the complete set of video processing tools for the Tennis domain has been introduced, starting from shot segmentation and classification, through player segmentation and tracking, to feature extraction. A number of experiments with HMMs have been carried out in order to find which combination of features, but also which HMM parameters would give the best results. The results have proved that specific features, such as the skeleton and the pie features are of the greatest importance. The novel features, which have been introduced in the chapter, have increased the number and the percentage of accurately recognizable strokes. Furthermore, experimental results have demonstrated that our approach is promising to realize statistics of tennis games automatically, using ordinary TV broadcast videos.

The aim of the Formula 1 case study was to extract the video sequences that contain announcer's excited speech and Formula 1 highlights. In addition, the goal was to find a technique that can be effectively used in content-based video retrieval for fusing the evidence obtained from different media. In this case study, we have chosen for Bayesian networks as more general tools that could accomplish that task. The comparison of Bayesian and dynamic Bayesian networks, which have been used for the extraction of excited speech, has shown the advantage of DBNs over BNs. This confirms the fact that temporal dependencies are very important. Therefore, a video cannot be considered as a set of independent images (see Figure 5.12).

Next, we have carried out numerous experiments with different atemporal and temporal connections within BNs/DBNs. They have shown that the inference in BNs do not vary much with the change of atemporal connections. However, the chosen atemporal, but also temporal dependencies between the nodes of two consecutive time slices, have a strong influence on the results of DBN inference.

The selected DBN has been validated for the extraction of highlights in the particular domain of the Formula 1 TV program. We have based our analysis on the fusion of the evidence obtained from different information sources (audio, video, and text). Consequently, a robust feature and text extraction schemes have been introduced for the audio-visual analysis of our particular domain. Results that are obtained from the text detection and recognition algorithm provide important information about the winner of the race, classification in a specific lap, etc. In Chapter 6, we elaborate more on the retrieval of this information together with other extracted information.

The fusion of indications, which are obtained from the three different media, has resulted in much better characterization of Formula 1 races. The audio DBN was able to detect a great number of segments where announcer raised his voice (recall 81%), which correspond to only 50% of all interesting segments, i.e. highlights in the race. The integrated audio-visual DBN was able to correct the result and detect about 80% of all interesting segments in the race. However, the audio part is still useful for the detection of the segments with the excited announcer speech, where it showed high recognition accuracy.

REFERENCES

[1] G. Sudhir, J. Lee, A. Jain, "Automatic Classification of Tennis Video for High-level Content-based Retrieval", In *Proceedings of IEEE Workshop on Content-based Access and Image and Video Databases*, Bombay, India, 1998, pp. 81-90.

[2] J. Yamato, J. Ohya, K. Ishii, "Recognizing Human Action in Time-Sequential Images Using Hidden Markov Model", In *Proceedings of the IEEE International Conference on Computer Vision and Pattern Recognition*, 1992, pp. 379-385.

[3] M. Naphade, T. Kristjansson, B. Frey, T.S. Huang, "Probabilistic multimedia objects (multijects): A novel approach to indexing and retrieval in multimedia systems", In *Proceedings of the IEEE International Conference on Image Processing (ICIP)*, Chicago, IL, 1998, vol. 3, pp. 536-540.

[4] Mitrovic D., "Machine Learning for Car Navigation", *Proc. 14th Int. Conference on Industrial and Engineering Applications of Artificial Intelligence and Expert Systems IEA/AIE-2001*, Budapest, June 2001, L. Monostori, J. Vancza and M. Ali (eds), Springer-Verlag, LNAI 2070, pp. 670-675.

[5] D. Moore, I. Essa, M. Hayes, "Exploiting Human Actions and Object Context for Recognition Tasks", In *Proceedings of the IEEE International Conference on Computer Vision (ICCV)*, vol. 1, Corfu, Greece, 1999, pp. 80-86.

[6] N. Vasconcelos, A. Lippman, "Bayesian Modeling of video editing and structure: Semantic features for video summarization and browsing", In *Proceeding of the IEEE International Conference on Image Processing (ICIP)*, vol. 2, Chicago, IL, 1998, pp. 550-555.

[7] A.M. Ferman, A.M. Tekalp, "Probabilistic Analysis and Extraction of Video Content", In *Proceedings of the IEEE International Conference on Image Processing (ICIP)*, vol. 2, Tokyo, Japan, 1999, pp. 91-95.

[8] T. Syeda-Mahmood, S. Srinivasan, "Detecting Topical Events in Digital Video", In *Proceedings of ACM Multimedia International Conference*, Los Angeles, CA, 2000, pp. 85-94.

[9] M. Naphade, T. S. Huang, "A Probabilistic Framework for Semantic Video Indexing, Filtering and Retrieval", *IEEE Transaction on Multimedia*, Vol 3, No. 1, March 2001.

[10] R.S. Jasinschi, N. Dimitrova, T. McGee, L. Agnihotri, J. Zimmerman, D. Li, "Integrated Multimedia Processing for Topic Segmentation and Classification", In *the Proceedings of IEEE Intl. Conf. on Image Processing (ICIP)*, Greece, 2001.

[11] M.Petkovic, W. Jonker, Z. Zivkovic, "Recognizing Strokes in Tennis Videos Using Hidden Markov Models", In *the Proceedings of the International Conference on Visualization, Imaging and Image Processing*, Marbella, Spain, 2001, pp. 512-516.

[12] M. Petkovic, V. Mihajlovic, W. Jonker, "Multi-Modal Extraction of Highlights from TV Formula 1 Programs", In *the Proceedings of the IEEE Intl. Conference on Multimedia and Expo (ICME)*, Lausanne, Switzerland, 2002.

[13] L. R. Rabiner, B.H. Juang, "An Introduction to Hidden Markov Models", *IEEE ASSP Magazine*, January 1986.

[14] L. Baum, T. Petrie, G. Soules, N. Weiss, "A maximization technique occurring in the statistical analysis of probabilistic functions of Markov chains", *Annals of Mathematical Statistics*, 41(1), 1970, pp. 164-171.

[15] T. Starner, J. Weaver, A. Pentland, "Real-time American Sign Language Recognition Using Desk and Wearable Computer Based Video", *Pattern Recognition and Machine Intelligence IEEE Transaction on*, 20(12), 1998, pp. 1371-1375.

[16] S. Muller, S. Eickeler, G. Rigoll, "Pseudo 3-D HMMs for Image Sequence Recognition", In *Proc. of the IEEE International Conference on Image Processing (ICIP)*, Tokyo, Japan, 1999, pp. 237-241.

[17] S. Michaelson, M. Steedman, *Hidden Markov Models for Speech Recognition*, Edinburgh University Press, 1990.

[18] F. Jensen, *An Introduction to Bayesian Networks*, Springer-Verlag, 1996.

[19] D. Heckerman, "A Tutorial on Learning Bayesian Networks", *Microsoft Research Technical Report*, MSR-TR-95-06, 1995.

[20] X. Boyen, N.Fiderman, D. Koller, "Discovering the Hidden Structure of Complex Dynamic Systems", In *Proceedings of International Conference on Uncertainty in Artificial Intelligence*, 1999, pp. 91-100.

[21] Z. Ghahramani, "Learning Dynamic Bayesian Networks", In *Adaptive Processing of Temporal Information* (C. L. Giles, M. Gori, eds.), Lecture Notes in Artificial Intelligence, Springer-Verlag, 1997.

[22] J. Pearl, *Probabilistic Reasoning in Intelligent Systems*, Morgan Kaufmann Publishers, 1988.

[23] V. Mihajlovic, M. Petkovic, *Dynamic Bayesian Networks: A State of the Art*, TR-CTIT-01-34, 2001.

[24] Z. Zivkovic, F. van der Heijden, M. Petkovic, W. Jonker, "Image processing and feature extraction for recognizing strokes in tennis game videos", In *the Proceedings of the Seventh Annual Conference of the Advanced School for Computing and Imaging*, the Netherlands, June 2001.

[25] A. Rosenfeld (ed.), *Multiresolution image processing and analysis*, Springer-Verlag, 1984.

[26] G. Johansson, "Visual perception of biological motion and a model for its analysis". *Perception and Psychoph.* 14(2), pp. 210-11, 1973.

[27] H. Fujiyoshi and A. Lipton, "Real-time Human Motion Analysis by Image Skeletonization" *IEEE Workshop on Applications of Computer Vision (WACV)*, Princeton NJ, pp. 15-21, 1998.

[28] R. Rosales and S. Sclaroff, "Inferring Body Pose without Tracking Body Parts", In *Proceedings of IEEE International Conference on Computer Vision and Pattern Recognition (CVPR)*, 2000.

[29] R. Duda, R. Hart, *Pattern Classification and Scene Analysis*, John Wiley, 1973.

[30] J. Yandell, *Visual Tennis*, Human Kinetics, 1999.

[31] T-L. Liu, D. Geiger, "Approximate Tree Matching and Shape Similarity", In *the Proceedings of the 7th International Conference on Computer Vision*, Greece, 1999, pp. 456-462.

[32] G. Pingali, Y. Jean, A. Opalach, I. Carlbom, "LucentVision: Converting Real World Events into Multimedia Experiences" In *Proceeding of the IEEE International Conference on Multimedia and Expo (ICME)*, New York City, vol.3, pp. 1433 -1436, 2000.

[33] V. Mihajlovic, M. Petkovic, *Automatic Annotation of Formula 1 Races for Content-based Video Retrieval*, Technical Report, *TR-CTIT-01-41*, 2001.

[34] W. Hess, *Pitch Determination of Speech Signal*, Springer-Verlag, New York, 1983.

[35] L. Rabiner, B.-H. *Jang, Fundamentals of Speech Recognition*, Englewood Cliffs, Prentice Hall, New York, 1993.

[36] J. Christie, *Completion of TNO-Abbot Research Project*, Technical Report Cambridge University, Cambridge, England, December 1996.

[37] X. Boyen, D. Koller, "Tractable Inference for Complex Stochastic Processes," In *Proceedings of the 14th Conference on Uncertainty in Artificial Intelligence*, Morgan Kaufmann Publishers, 1998.

Chapter 6

COBRA: A PROTOTYPE OF A VIDEO DBMS

1. INTRODUCTION

An increasing number of large video libraries, which are becoming publicly available, result in a demand for techniques that can manipulate the video data based on content. This has led to a wide range of research on techniques for video database management systems (see [1-4] for reviews). However, a traditional database management system does not provide enough facilities for managing and retrieving video contents. Therefore, in the preceding chapters, we have recommended some solutions for the major problems. First, we have proposed a suitable video framework and then several knowledge-based methods for interpreting raw data into semantic content.

Throughout this book a lot of video retrieval systems that offer a sort of content-based retrieval have been surveyed. However, as they mainly come from the computer vision community, they have problems with scalability, because they were only intended for small collections of data. Furthermore, they stick to one technique for semantic content extraction. On the other hand, we can see from the Tennis case study that a combination of different techniques is indispensable. In fact, the selection of the technique to be used depends on the type of events to be extracted (for example, in our approach, spatio-temporal formalization is applied for the net-playing event, but hidden Markov models for stroke recognition).

Therefore, we propose an approach that integrates different techniques used for content-based retrieval within a DBMS [5]. Furthermore, we introduce a general DBMS architecture, which can be efficiently used for content-based video retrieval in different domains. This chapter presents a prototype of a video database management system, which implements that architecture and most of our ideas.

Firstly, we implement the proposed Cobra framework within a DBMS. Then, the video processing and feature extraction techniques are integrated into the DBMS, which allows incremental and dynamical change of metadata. Furthermore, we integrate into the system a few knowledge-based techniques, namelý hidden Markov models, Dynamic Bayesian Networks (DBNs), and our spatio-temporal approach. We demonstrate how these techniques can be used together to automatically interpret low-level features into semantic content. By coupling these techniques with the DBMS tightly and by integrating them in all three layers of the DBMS architecture (not only in one place), we achieve a high degree of scalability, flexibility, and efficiency.

Although our approach benefits of using domain knowledge, it also provides a general framework that can efficiently use the aforementioned techniques in different domains.

The remainder of this chapter is structured as follows. First, we present the architecture of the prototype of a video database management system in Section 2. Next, in Section 3 we describe the system implementation giving more details about the implementation platform and developed extensions. Section 4 is dedicated to the integration of video processing and feature extraction techniques within the DBMS. An approach that facilitates off-line extraction of metadata is presented in Section 5. In Section 6, we describe the integration of hidden Markov models within the DBMS, as well as parallel inference. The advantages of integrated querying are demonstrated in Section 7. In Section 8, we describe a search engine, which integrates our system, providing means for searching digital libraries, intranets, and web-based document collections. Finally, Section 9 summarizes the chapter and brings conclusions.

2. ARCHITECTURE OF THE COBRA VDBMS

The architecture of our video DBMS is designed to be easily extensible, supporting the use of different knowledge-based techniques for the derivation of the video content. The features and content abstractions, which are stored as metadata, are used to organize, index, and retrieve the video source. The metadata is populated off-line most of the time using *feature extractors* and *semantic discovery engines* (Figure 6.1), but can also be extracted at query time (dynamic extraction).

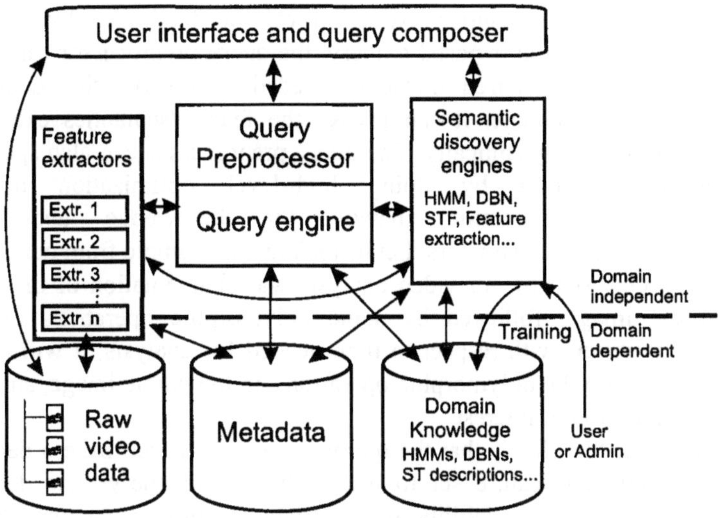

Figure 6.1. The conceptual architecture

To achieve content independence, we have introduced a video data framework, called Cobra, in Chapter 3. The framework supports the automatic extraction of high-level concepts (objects and events) from raw video data. It is independent of feature/semantic extractors, providing flexibility in using different video processing and pattern recognition techniques for these purposes. The framework distinguishes four distinct layers within video content: the raw data, the feature, the object, and the event layer. The object and event layers are concept layers consisting of entities characterized by prominent spatial and temporal dimensions, respectively. By using the Cobra video framework, we achieve insulation between applications and feature/semantics extraction techniques on the one hand, and data on the other hand.

As already mentioned, the framework is flexible in using different knowledge-based techniques for interpreting raw video data into high-level concepts. For that purpose, our prototype VDBMS can use various methods described in the preceding chapters, such as Hidden Markov Models (HMMs), Dynamic Bayesian Networks (DBNs), spatio-temporal formalization, but it is not only limited to these techniques. It can be easily extended to support neural networks, entropy maximization, or some other techniques. From the implementation point of view, flexibility is achieved by choosing an open and flexible database kernel that is easy to extend in order to support different semantics extraction techniques. The next section elaborates more on that.

Dynamic feature/semantics extraction can be facilitated by a *query preprocessor*. Once a user posed a query, the query preprocessor can check the availability of required metadata needed to resolve this query. If metadata is not available, it can invoke the feature/semantics extraction engines to obtain it dynamically. The query preprocessor can also speed up the query execution by doing high-level optimization of the feature/semantics extraction, having the knowledge about the implementation of the extractors. Let us look at the example from our Tennis case study. One step of our video analysis was segmentation of the lower part of the image, followed by some polymorphic operations on this segment. However, with respect to time needed for analysis, it will not be the same if we do the polymorphic operations on the whole image, and then segment our region of interest.

In addition, the idea is that the query preprocessor can make a decision which method and feature set to use to fulfill the query. The decision depends on the (un)availability of metadata (features/semantics already extracted) and methods for feature/semantics extraction, as well as on the cost and quality models of these methods. Let us look again at the Tennis case study and stroke recognition. Suppose that the query preprocessor has to resolve an ad-hoc query, which involves stroke recognition. Presume that not all features described in the stroke recognition experiments had been extracted, particularly the features that give the best result. Having a precision table (e.g. Table 5.2), the query preprocessor can make a trade-off between the time needed for the extraction of features that will give the best result and a lower precision of stroke recognition obtained by using a combination of features that had been already extracted.

As shown in Figure 6.1, domain independence of our approach is achieved by separating *domain knowledge* and techniques that use it. Domain knowledge is stored within the database. Therefore, the system can be used in different domains. To provide a user with the ability to query a new domain, knowledge of that domain, i.e. hidden Markov models, structures of dynamic Bayesian networks with probability distributions, or spatio-temporal event descriptions, has to be provided. In addition to general feature extractors, some domains will require specific ones as well, which should be provided.

However, in practice, multimedia data is very often distributed. This is often due to the need for big storage capacity, but also because of the nature of data sources. Subsequently, this implies the necessity for distributed query processing. With respect to this problem, we suggest the architecture presented in Figure 6.2. In comparison to the architecture presented in Figure 6.1, this distributed database management system has a central directory that stores metadata and it has distributed Content Extraction

Servers (CESs) that are close to multimedia raw data. CESs are responsible for video processing, feature/semantics extraction, and video streaming. They include semantic discovery engines that derive video content representation using HMMs or DBNs. Instead of distributing only data, this schema distributes the modules that operate on that data.

As a new video arrives in a multimedia data collection, predefined features and concepts are extracted by the corresponding CES and stored in the central directory. Consequently, a user's query is usually resolved in the central directory using features and concepts that are already extracted from raw data (solid lines in Figure 6.2). However, if the query comprises some features or concepts that are not already extracted, the central directory sends a request to corresponding CES(s) to extract features/concepts at run time.

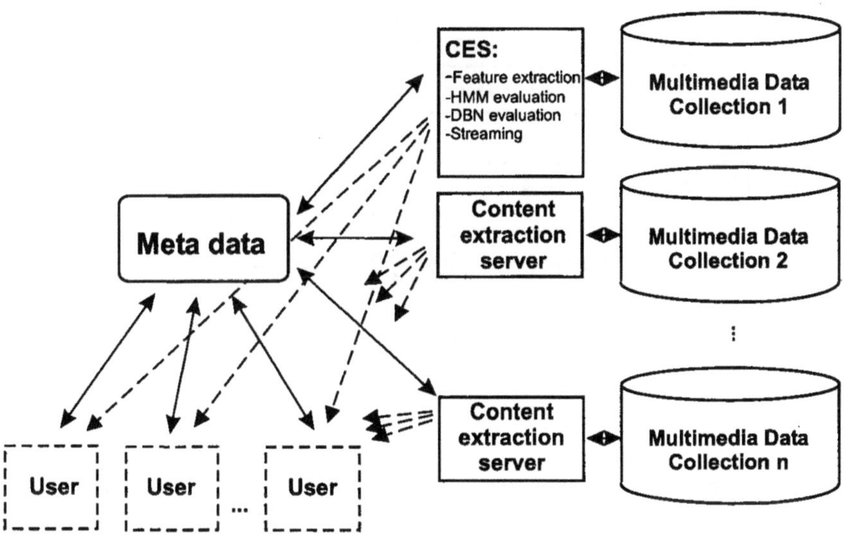

Figure 6.2. A distributed architecture

When a user want to see actual videos, which are the results of his queries, the central directory forwards a request to the corresponding CES(s). A streaming server, which is included in each CES, streams the requested (part of) video directly to the user (dashed lines in Figure 6.2).

Furthermore, this architecture is also very suitable for the parallelization of query processing, being able to distribute a job to many CESs that can work in parallel. Even more, the number of CESs can exceed greatly the number of storage places, i.e. one storage place can be coupled with many CESs.

3. IMPLEMENTATION PLATFORM

The main ideas of the architecture, which are presented in the previous section, are implemented within our prototype video database system that follows the well-known three-level DBMS architecture (Figure 6.3).

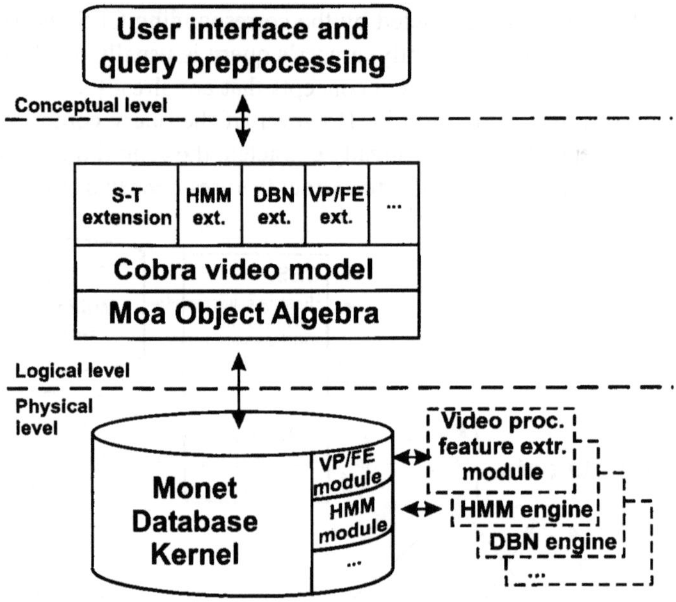

Figure 6.3. The Cobra VDBMS

At the *conceptual level*, the prototype implements a graphical query interface and a query preprocessor. The query interface is used to support graphically the formalization of a user query. A detailed description, which is supported by an example query, is given in Section 6. Although the query preprocessor is intended to organize and optimize dynamic feature extraction by performing preprocessing described in the previous section, in the current implementation it only rewrites a graphical query into the Moa or SQL query.

The Moa object algebra [6], enriched with the types and operators defined in the Cobra video model, as well as in several extensions, is used at the *logical level*. The algebra accepts all base types of the underlying physical storage system and allows their orthogonal combination using the structure primitives: set, tuple, and object. This provides data independence between the logical and physical level, as well as extra optimization possibilities during query execution.

At the logical level, we define structures and operators that support Moa extensions. In the current implementation, we have three extensions: Video-processing/feature-extraction, HMM, and the spatio-temporal extension. In the following, we will describe them briefly, whereas the next three sections will bring more details about them.

The video-processing and feature-extraction extension encapsulates operations used for video segmentation, processing, and feature extraction. Operations are implemented using Matlab and its image processing toolbox and as such used through a Matlab server directly by the DBMS. We use the same Matlab server to work with dynamic Bayesian networks, since the DBN learning and inference algorithms are implemented in Matlab.

The spatio-temporal extension is tightly coupled with the system. It is implemented within the query engine. It is aimed at formalizing the descriptions of high-level concepts, as well as their extraction based on features and spatio-temporal reasoning.

The HMM extension integrates HMM techniques used for the extraction of semantics within our system. It implements two basic HMM operations: training and evaluation. This provides a user with the ability to train new models by choosing the training data set directly form the database. Furthermore, the user can evaluate these new models against the data in the database dynamically (at query time).

Let us go back to the implementation of our prototype. For each Moa operation, there is a program written using an interface language understood by the *physical layer*. In this implementation of our prototype, a Moa query is rewritten into Monet Interface Language (MIL), which is understood by Monet [7] – an extensible parallel database kernel that is used at the physical level. Note that the system can use different database kernels at physical level. Monet supports a binary relational model, main memory query execution, extensibility with Abstract Data Types (ADTs), and new index structures, as well as parallelism. For a short description of Monet see Chapter 2, or [7] for a detailed one.

The Moa extensions are also supported at the physical level by the efficient implementation of their operations. In our prototype, the operations of the extensions are implemented as Monet functions using MIL and MEL[1] modules.

The integration of several knowledge-based techniques within the VDBMS by extending our system at all levels results in the preserving of data and application independence. This is an important advantage over approaches that implement a video extension at the application level because it results in a much flexible system.

[1] Monet Extension Language

4. DYNAMIC FEATURE EXTRACTION

The video-processing and feature-extraction extension encapsulates operations used for video processing, segmentation, and feature extraction. Examples of these operations are: the extraction of color histograms, region segmentation, and shot segmentation, among many others.

These operations are implemented using Matlab and its toolboxes. This eases the process of their implementation because a developer has at his disposal rich Matlab libraries that support video and image processing. Furthermore, this allows the easy extending of the system by adding new feature extractors as Matlab operations. Finally, it corresponds to the architecture presented in Figure 6.2, supporting the parallelization of feature/semantics extraction process that is very time-consuming.

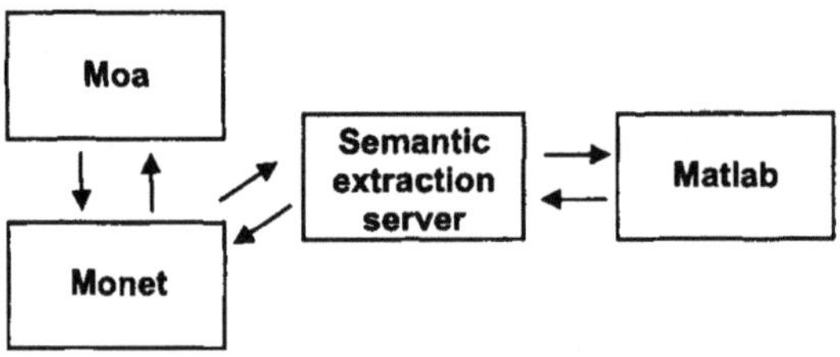

Figure 6.4. Feature extraction using Matlab

Within a DBMS, the definitions of new operations are added at the physical level and accepted automatically by logical and conceptual levels. However, they are resolved by a Content Extraction Server (CES) and the corresponding Matlab functions as shown in Figure 6.4. A real example is given in Figure 6.5. The Moa query selects all frame sequences which frames have a dominant color less than 120. The query can be used for example as a very simple segmentation function. The dominant color function is propagated to the Monet level where an interface to Matlab is implemented using MIL (Fig. 6.5b). The interface sends a remote call using the TCP/IP module of Monet to a CES (Fig. 6.5c). The CES prepares raw video data for processing and invokes the corresponding function implemented in Matlab to extract the dominant color. The Matlab function does all computations and then retrieves results via the CES back to Monet. The results are consequently propagated to the logical and conceptual level.

The presented approach allows dynamic feature extraction, which is in some cases very important. It can be applied in the area of video mining in cases when some very rarely used features are used for answering mining queries. It is not sufficient to have these features, which will be used only once, stored permanently, as they can occupy very large space.

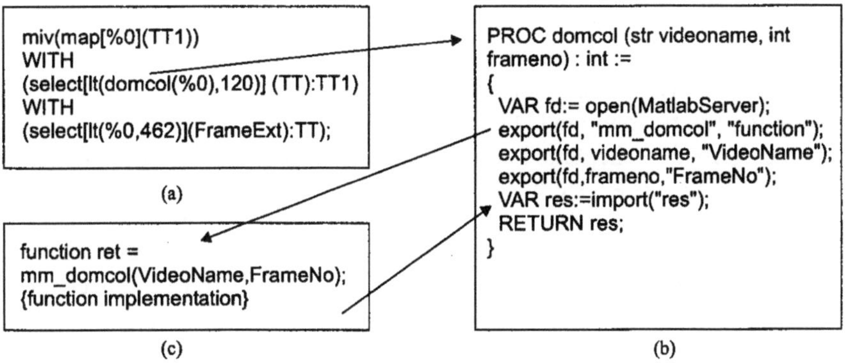

Figure 6.5. Implementation of the dominant color function: (a) Moa level, (b) Monet level, (c) Matlab

Dynamic feature extraction is advantageous for applications where costs for the extracting features at run time are less than costs for their storage. Nowadays, this can be the case for very simple features, which extraction is not time consuming. However, with emerging in computer technology, processors and specialized hardware will be capable to extract in run time more and more complicated features very soon. Finally, dynamic feature/semantics extraction is indispensable for the whole group of video monitoring/surveillance applications where real-time or near real-time processing is needed.

5. OFF-LINE METADATA EXTRACTION USING FEATURE GRAMMARS

Although dynamic feature extraction can be useful, in most cases video processing and feature extraction are done off-line. The reason is that these processes deal with enormous quantities of data, which processing is still very time-consuming. In addition, they often produce massive quantities of results (features). Therefore, even the off-line video processing and feature extraction can be incredibly complex and unmanageable. Consequently, a flexible solution for extraction of metadata from raw video data is very important. In this section, we show how a feature grammar [8] can be used to manage the feature extraction process in the Tennis case study.

The feature grammars form the core of a system for indexing multimedia data, called Acoi [9]. They are based on the theory of context-free grammars [10], intended to describe the relationships between metadata and detectors (video processing functions and feature extractors) in the set of grammar rules. For a detailed description of feature grammars, we refer to [8, 9]. In the sequel, we describe an instantiation of our Cobra framework for the Tennis case study, which is formed using feature grammars. A more detailed description can be found in [11].

As described in chapters 4 and 5, video processing and feature extraction in the Tennis case study comprises different steps, such as shot segmentation, classification, the extraction of different features, etc. All these processes are done by different algorithms. The Tennis feature grammar, which was developed for the case study, describes the execution order and dependences among these extraction algorithms. So managing the metadata is now done by exploiting the dependencies in the feature grammar. The dependencies among the processes of the tennis video analysis are shown in Figure 6.6.

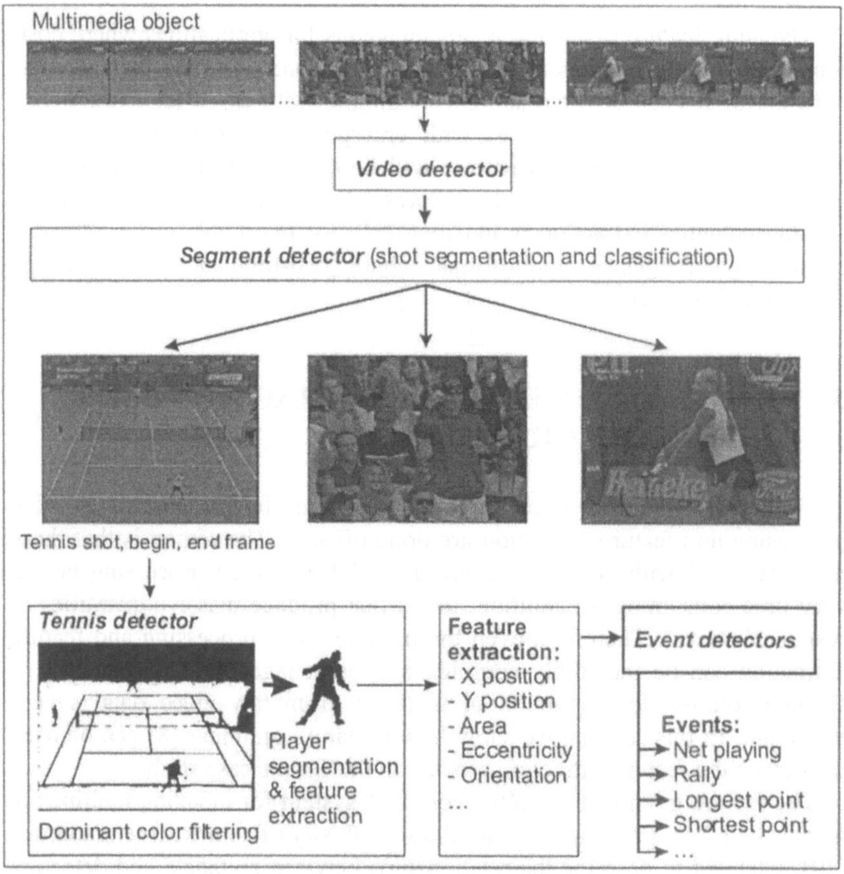

Figure 6.6. Detector dependencies

To populate the meta-data the feature grammar is used to generate a parser: the Feature Detector Engine (FDE). This FDE triggers the execution of the associated detectors. In the remainder, we will describe the detection steps.

After finding a video object, the Tennis FDE executes the segment detector. This detector, which is implemented externally, segments the video into different shots. The shot boundaries are detected using differences in color histograms of neighboring frames[2]. The same algorithm encapsulates shot classification. It classifies shots in four different categories: playing, close-up, audience, and other. If the segment detector classifies a shot as a playing shot, the Tennis FDE starts execution of the tennis detector. Its task is to segment and track the tennis player. Next, the algorithm that extracts features characterizing the shape of the segmented player's binary representation is invoked. Besides the players' position, this algorithm extracts the dominant color, and standard shape features, such as the mass center, the area, the bounding box, the orientation, and the eccentricity.

Furthermore, the feature grammar can also be used to specify some simple event rules. These rules are then called white-box detectors in contrast to black-box detectors (all the algorithms described above), which are implemented externally and are not part of the grammar. In our case study, player's positions and their transitions over time are related to particular events (net-playing, rally, etc.) using rules. These rules, which use spatio-temporal relations, are implemented as white- and black-box detectors within the FDE. The definition of the net-playing rule, which is implemented as a white-box detector, is given in Figure 6.7, as an example.

```
% detector        netplay some[tennis.frame] (
                      player.yPos <= 170.0 );
```

Figure 6.7. The definition of the net-playing rule

Using this data-driven approach metadata can be extracted off-line without any intervention by an operator. However, this off-line, static specification of events that are extracted from video has some drawbacks. Let us consider the specification of the net playing rule within the grammar. It just checks if the y coordinate of player's position is less than 170 (Figure 6.7). However, a user, such as a tennis coach, might want to change the

[2] This algorithm and the algorithms mentioned in the following text are described in chapters 3, 4, and 5.

threshold or to see only the fragments where the player overlaps with the net for example. To be able to immediately see the result sequences, he needs a run time answer to his query. This will be dealt with in the next section.

6. SPATIO-TEMPORAL EXTENSION

In this section, we discuss the implementation that had to be done to extend the database management system, e.g. the Moa/Monet platform, to be able to model and query events using spatio-temporal relations in run time. In order to achieve the automatic extraction of events using the event grammar, we had to define a basic set of spatio-temporal relations at the Moa level. As far as spatial relations are concerned, we use the Minimum Bounding Rectangle (MBR) approximation of the object geometry in order to retrieve the potential objects efficiently. Based on that, we implemented fundamental topological relations (equal, inside, cover, overlap, touch, disjoint, and two inverse covered_by and contains) and the three distance relation from the set σ. Definitions of these relations, as well as interval temporal relations are given in Chapter 4. Extensibility of the database platform allows users to define specific relations based on this minimal set, such as going towards, opposite, away from, etc.

As far as temporal relations are concerned, we defined point and interval data type to represent frames and frame sequences respectively. There is a relationship between each concept (object or event) and a set of intervals, i.e. frame sequences, where it occurs. We also defined the basic relations of interval and point temporal algebra, the mapping between them with aggregates that operate on sets such as 'make intervals', 'start interval', 'end interval', as well as operations on the interval data type such as duration, intersect, and union.

The 'make intervals' is a set aggregate operation that is used to generate frame sequences from frame numbers. As we want to allow combinations of spatial relations, which are related to one frame, and the temporal relations of the interval algebra that span over frames, within one query, such an operation is indispensable. A query example with a description of its processing will be given at the end of this section.

The "make interval" operation converts frame numbers (time slices) into frame sequences (time intervals). Figure 6.8 shows the source code of this operation. The Java procedure, shown in the upper part of Figure 6.8, extends the Moa rewriter, while the MIL procedure, shown at the bottom part, is used for making intervals at the physical level. The Moa procedure sorts the input frames and then calls the MIL procedure, which transforms frames into intervals in the way that the start of an interval is in the head column, while the end is in the tail column of the output BAT. Finally, the Moa procedure creates a tuple from the head and tail part of the BAT retrieved by the MIL procedure.

```
private Structure mintervals(MOAdd dd,Expression expr) throws RewriteException {
    MILexpr startiv, endiv, ividx;
    MILexpr res = MILop.reverse( new MILop( keyTable(), "NILcast", getValues() ) );
    res = MILop.reverse( MILop.sort(res) ); // sort the input data
    res = new MILop( keyTable(), "miv", res ); // make the intervals (batloop)
    endiv = MILop.nilcast( res );
    startiv = MILop.reverse( MILop.castnil( res ) );
    ividx = MILop.mirror( startiv );
    Expression tAttrs[] = {new AtomicIVS( startiv ), new AtomicIVS( endiv ) };
    Expression sAttrs[] = {ividx, Rewriter.rewrite( dd, new Constructor( keyTable(),
         "TUPLE", tAttrs ) ) };
    Structure result = Rewriter.rewrite( dd, new Constructor( keyTable(),
         "SET", sAttrs ) );
    return ((Structure)(expr.substitute(result))); }

PROC miv(BAT[void,int] inbat) : BAT[int,int] := {
    VAR res := new(int,int); VAR initial := true;
    VAR first := nil; VAR curr := nil; VAR prev := nil;
    inbat @ batloop() {
      IF (initial) {first := $t; prev := first; initial := false; }
      ELSE {curr := $t; IF (curr != prev+1) {res.insert(first,prev);
           first := curr; }prev := curr; }
    }
    res.insert(first,curr);
    RETURN res; }
```

Figure 6.8. Source of the 'make intervals' operation

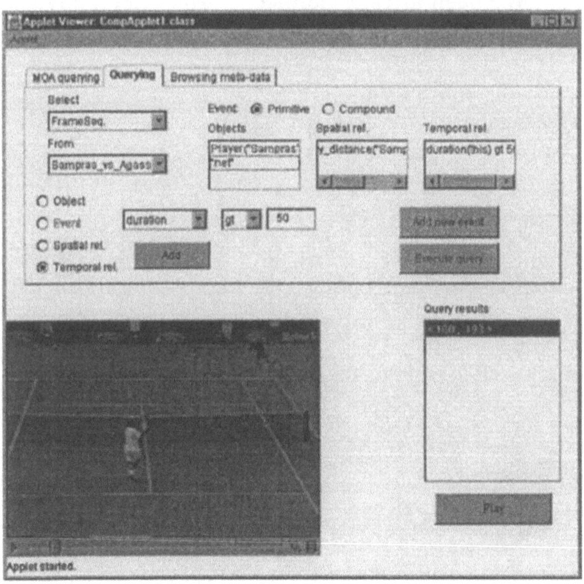

Figure 6.9. The user interface for event descriptions

In order to provide a user with means to describe semantic events interactively on a screen, a graphical user interface is developed. Let us take the net playing query as an example to show how an event should be defined (see Figure 6.9). A user can choose a type that will be retrieved as a result of a query (frame sequences in the case of our query example). Then, the user can specify a video file and a category of the event that he wants to describe. Next, he adds objects that are involved in this event type and selects spatial and temporal relations among objects (in this case the distance and duration relations). After posing a query, the query composer rewrites it and manages its processing. As an illustration, the net-playing query, after rewriting into the Moa object algebra and consequently into the Monet Interface Language (MIL), is given in Figure 6.10a and 6.10b, respectively. Note that Figure 6.10b shows only a small part of the very large MIL graph. The video sequences that satisfy the query criteria are then listed in the query result box. The user can play a sequence by selecting it from the list. For that purpose, a Java Media Framework player is integrated in the tool. The user can also update metadata by adding the newly defined event in the database, which will allow him later to define more complex compound events that comprise this event. This will also speed up the future querying of this event, because the query will be resolved in the event layer without looking at other layers. In addition, the user is able to browse metadata discovering objects and events that have been already defined. Furthermore, advanced users are able to specify complex Moa queries directly.

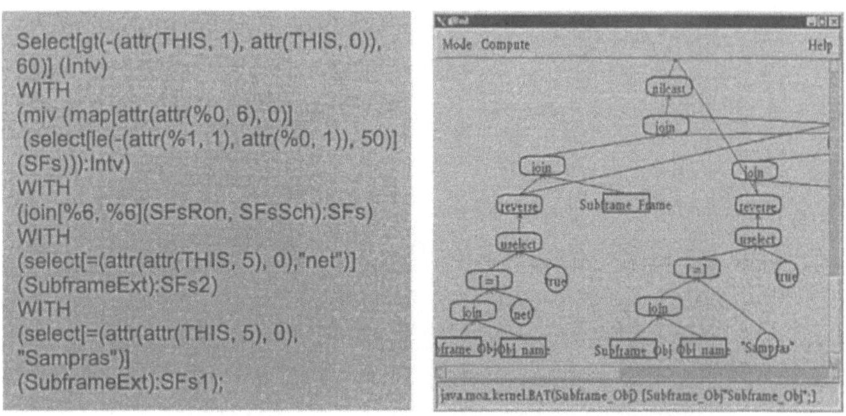

(a) (b)

Figure 6.10. The net-playing query: a) Moa; b) a part of the MIL graph

To show the importance of the 'make interval' operation, let us consider the processing of spatio-temporal event descriptions. In general, it follows one of two approaches described in Figure 6.11. If there is a common operand between the spatial and the temporal part of the query, which is more often the case, the evaluation shown in Figure 6.11a is performed. Let us look back at the 'net playing' query (Figure 6.10a). First, the sub-frames that represent Sampras and the net are selected and joined (bottom part of Figure 6.10a). Then, the query is restricted on only sub-frame tuples that satisfy the spatial operator distance (line 5). We project the frame numbers and perform the 'make intervals' (miv) operation to get a set of video intervals as the result (line 4). Finally, the intervals that satisfied the temporal condition, i.e. ones that are longer than specified threshold, are selected (line 1).

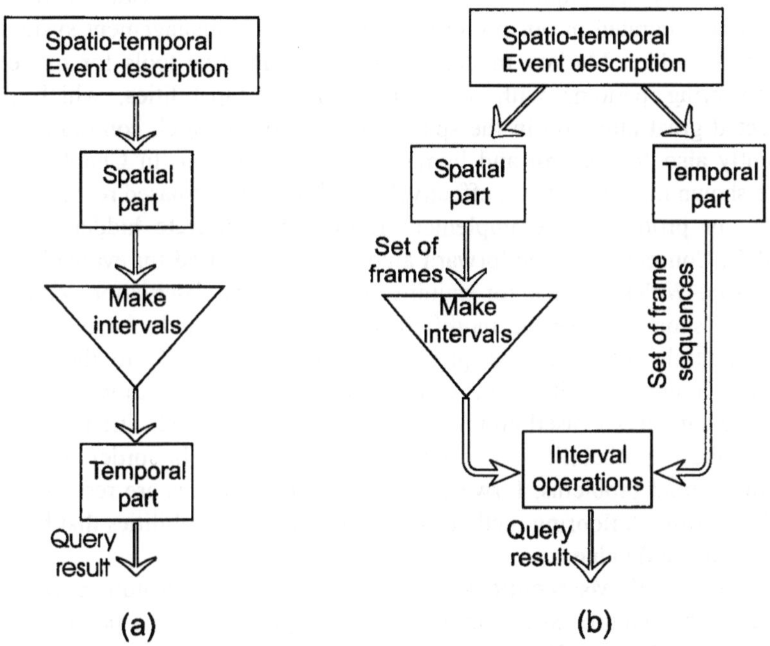

Figure 6.11. Examples of query evaluation: (a) sequential evaluation; (b) parallel evaluation

Otherwise, if there is no common operand between the spatial and the temporal part, the system can perform parallel evaluation shown in Figure 6.11b. In this case, for the spatial part it first looks at the set of objects and throws away all objects that are not involved in spatial operations. Then, spatial operations are evaluated on remained objects using the sub-frame class, which stores the spatial data. Finally, the system performs a projection over the target list to obtain frame numbers. A similar process is performed for the temporal part of the event description. However, as the evaluation of the temporal part of the query has been done using interval temporal algebra, the result is a set of intervals that represents the required frame sequences. Hence, we have to convert frame numbers into intervals (frame sequences) in order to match the result of the spatial part of the query with the temporal part. This is done again by the 'make intervals' operation. Depending on the relations between the spatial and the temporal part, an interval operation (intersect or union) is performed on these two sets of intervals.

7. HMM INTEGRATION

One of the techniques for the automatic extraction of video semantics, which is integrated in our prototype video database management system, is based on hidden Markov models. HMMs are effective tools for modeling time-varying patterns with automatic learning capabilities, which have attracted great attention in the speech recognition research community, but recently also for gesture and human action recognition. In Chapter 5, we have shown that they can be effectively used for content-based retrieval.

In our prototype, we implement left-to-right, discrete hidden Markov models. Consequently, the forward algorithm [12] is used for evaluation and the Baum-Welch method for training. As the tennis observation sequences are very short, we use the modified re-estimation formula for the training with multiple observation sequences given in Chapter 5. In the training process, a number of iterations of the Baum-Welch algorithm with different initial parameters is used aiming at finding the best model. The model with the highest probability is chosen as the result. In order to avoid computational problems, forward and backward variables are rescaled after each iteration. A flooring method is used to replace probabilities that become zero with small value ε.

Discrete HMMs require translation of continuous feature parameters (obtained by feature extraction module) into symbols from a predefined set (codebook). A few MIL functions are implemented for clusterization and quantization. Having the cluster centers and an observation sequence of features, the distances between the feature tuple and all cluster centers are calculated. The tuple is substituted by the symbol, which belongs to the cluster with the minimum distance from its center to the observation vector. The computation is adjusted for the BAT algebra that is used in Monet.

In the database, we model the discrete HMM as:

$$\lambda = (N, M, A, B, \pi, ID, Cen, \Sigma_E),$$

As already mentioned in Chapter 5, the first five elements of the tuple describe an HMM. The parameters N and M are the number of states and the number of observation symbols, respectively. The matrices A and B define the state transition and observation symbol probability distribution, respectively. The initial state distribution is denoted as π.

In addition to that, for each HMM, we store its ID, the event type for which the HMM is used, and a vector containing cluster centers Cen. Eventually, the accuracy of event recognition compared to human annotation of the example data set can be stored for each HMM. The accuracy can be initially obtained experimentally (as described in Chapter 5), and then can be calculated statistically using for example relevance feedback. As already mentioned, the optimizer and query preprocessor can use this information during query evaluation.

The HMM engine implements two basic operations for HMMs: evaluation and training.

For evaluation, i.e. calculating $P(O|\lambda)$ - the probability of a particular observation sequence O, being generated by the model with given parameters, we implement the operation hmm_evaluate(ID, O, T), where ID is the identification of the HMM and T is the length of the observation sequence O.

Training is a process of adjusting the model parameters to observed training data in order to maximize $P(O|\lambda)$. For that, we implement the hmm_train(N, M, O^T, L^T, T) operation, where O^T and L^T are the set of T observation sequences and the set of their individual lengths, respectively.

Our implementation of HMMs follows the approach used for the feature extraction extension. We add the operations mentioned above at the physical level of the database management system, but also extend the logical level. As a data-intensive process, quantization is implemented within Monet, while HMM evaluation and training are implemented within an HMM engine. The engine is remotely called from the DBMS using the TCP/IP module of Monet. The reason to have them separately is parallelization/distribution of these two very time consuming processes.

We exploit the parallelism of our database kernel and implement the parallel evaluation of different HMMs at the physical level. Figure 6.12 shows a database server with the HMM extension, which calls remotely six HMM engines performing parallel evaluation. In this way, we are able to perform parallel evaluation of strokes in our Tennis case study. Each class of strokes is represented by an HMM model. Six models are evaluated at a time and one with the highest probability is assigned to the evaluated stroke. By distributing the HMM evaluation, we speed up the query processing of the computing-intensive inference operation. The training operation can be parallelized in a similar way. A number of iterations are divided among accessible engines and the best model is chosen. Using parallelization, we significantly reduce the time needed for the training, as well as for the parallel evaluation process.

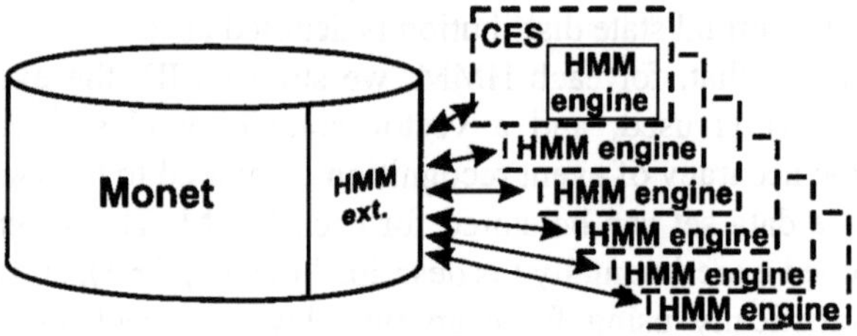

Figure 6.12. Parallel HMM inference

To be more specific, let us have a look at the HMM inference operator, which is at the Monet level implemented as a MIL function (Figure 6.13).

```
PROC hmmParallel(BAT[oid,dbl] f1, BAT[oid,dbl] f2, BAT[oid,dbl] f3,
 BAT[oid,dbl} f4) : str := {

  # preparing an observation sequence
  #(quantization of features)...
  VAR Obser:=new(void,int);
  Obser:=quant(f1,f2,f3,f4);
  VAR num:=howmany(f1);
  VAR parEval:=new(str,flt);

  # evaluating 6 models in parallel
  VAR ProcessNo:=threadcnt(7));
  {|

    # Service stroke
    VAR vr:=hmmOneCall(Server1, "aMatrixS.bat", "bMatrixS.bat", Obser, num);
    parEval.insert("Service",vr);

    # Forehand stroke
    vr:=hmmOneCall(server2, "aMatrixF.bat", "bMatrixF.bat", Obser, num);
    parEval.insert("Forehand",vr);

    # Smash stroke
    vr:=hmmOneCall(Server3, "aMatrixSm.bat", "bMatrixSm.bat", Obser, num);
    parEval.insert("Smash",vr);

    # Backhand stroke
    vr:=hmmOneCall1(Server4, "aMatrixB.bat", "bMatrixB.bat", Obser, num);
    parEval.insert("Backhand",vr);

    # Volley backhand stroke
    vr:=hmmOneCall1(Server5, "aMatrixVB.bat", "bMatrixVB.bat", Obser, num);
    parEval.insert("VolleyBackhand",vr);

    # Volley forehand stroke
    vr:=hmmOneCall1(Server6, "aMatrixVF.bat", "bMatrixVF.bat", Obser, num);
    parEval.insert("VolleyBackhand",vr);
  |}

  VAR hiPr:=parEval.max;
  VAR ret:=(parEval.reverse).find(hiPr);

  RETURN ret;
}
```

Figure 6.13. Parallel evaluation of 6 HMMs

The function uses the parallel execution operator of Monet. In that way, it sends data and starts evaluation of six HMM models on six different HMM engines in parallel. After obtaining results from all six engines, the procedure finds which one gives the maximum probability and returns it as the result.

At the logical level, we develop two functions for the evaluation of hidden Markov models. Figure 6.14 shows two Moa queries that use these functions.

```
hmmSetV(SET<ind12,SET<ind11,TUPLE<Atomic<fs1>,Atomic
<fs2>,Atomic<fs3>,Atomic<fs4>>,ind12>>);

    map[hmmSetIVS(THIS)](SET<ind12,SET<ind11,TUPLE<Atomic<fs
1>,Atomic<fs2>,Atomic<fs3>,Atomic<fs4>>,ind12>>;
```

Figure 6.14. Invoking HMM operations at the Moa level

8. INTEGRATED QUERYING

Some simple query examples have already been given in the previous chapters. Here, we will shortly revise the basic query capabilities of our system through a few plain examples and then concentrate on some more complex examples that show integrated use of different semantic description extraction techniques. Examples are taken from our two case studies.

The basic query facilities of the system imply querying features, objects, and events. Using a graphical user interface, a user can choose among those three possibilities. Then he can easily define a query by selecting particular features (objects or events) and by setting constraints on them. For example, a user can pose a query that selects all frames which dominant color is less than 120. The evaluation of this query has been explained in detail in Section 4.

In a similar way, a user can query objects and events. The example given in Section 5 (Figure 6.9) defines a new event using objects and their spatio-temporal relations. Here, we will give another example, which shows how a compound event can be defined based on already defined events (Figure 6.15).

The event grammar allows users to define their own events and build the metadata themselves. The example, which is shown in Figure 6.15, defines a new event called "rallies with net playing" by introducing overlap temporal operation between the "playing on the net" and "rally" events. After the evaluation of the query, results are added to the metadata. This speeds up further querying of this event, which is resolved directly in the event layer of metadata without performing costly join operation for resolving the temporal relation.

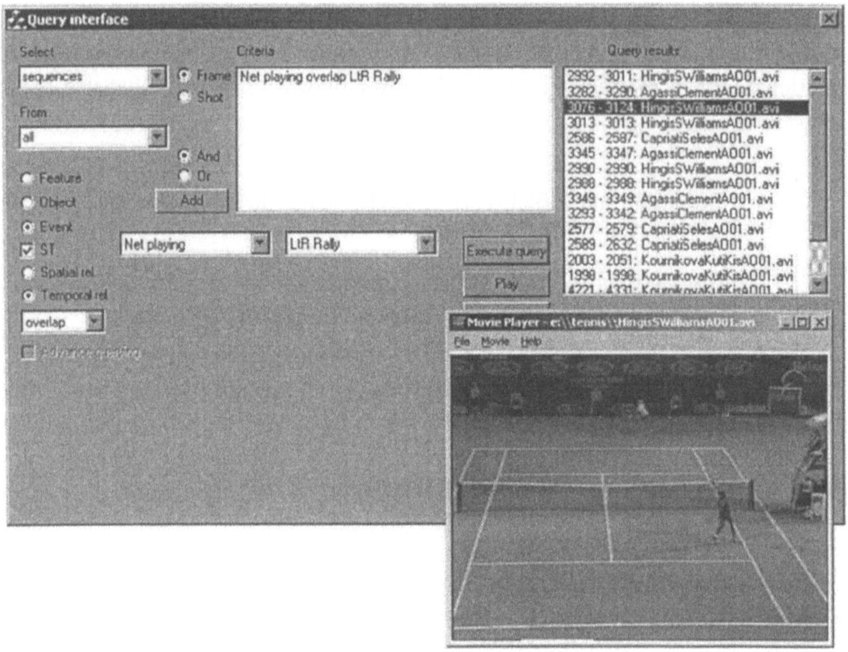

Figure 6.15. Compound events

One of the major advantages of the Cobra video framework is that it supports the integrated use of different techniques for the derivation of semantic content (a detailed description can be found in [13]). Therefore, we can benefit of using the spatio-temporal event formalization together with the stochastic formalization and answer very detailed complex queries, such as "Select all video sequences from the game between Kournikova and Kuti Kis with net playing and smashes". The query notation used in Chapter 4 and also below is replaced by the graphical query interface (see Figure 6.16).

```
SELECT vi.frame_seq
FROM video vi
WHERE s_contains (vi.frame_seq, event,
Smash_on_net = ({e1: Player_near_the_net,
e2: Smash}, {},{},{},
{overlap (e2, e1)},
e1.o1= e2.o1)) = 1 AND vi.name = 'KournikovaKutiKis'
```

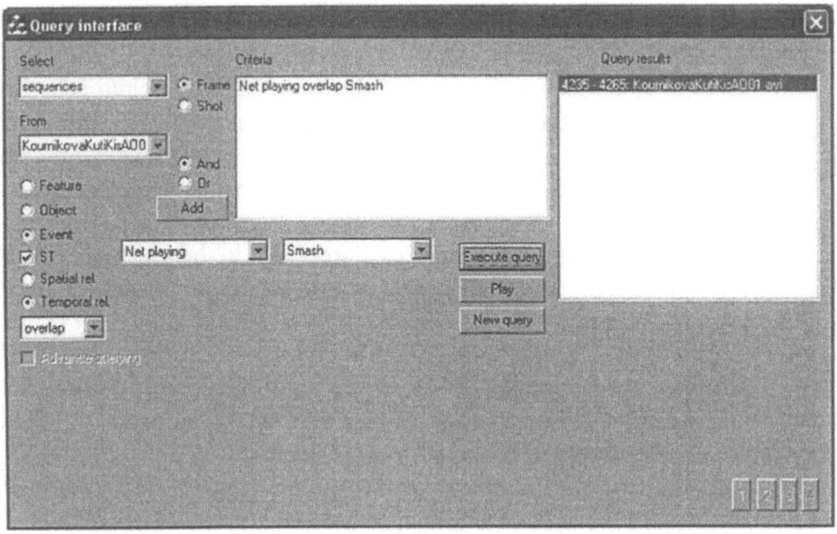

Figure 6.16. Graphical user interface for combined queries

Similarly to the previous example, this query comprises a new event type, in this case the "Smash_on_net" event that consists of two events. Note that these two primitive events are extracted using different methods for video event interpretation. The first one is the "Player_near_the_net" event, which is defined in Section 3.3 of Chapter 4 using the spatio-temporal formalization, while the second one, the "Smash" event, is defined in Section 4 of Chapter 5 using the HMM approach. For this new event type, we also have one temporal relation that requires the event e_1 to overlap with the event e_2.

Except for querying features, objects, and events separately, the model allows a user to combine these three levels of video metadata in one query. For example, the query "Select all close-up sequences of Martina Hingis with the court in background from the match Monica Seles – Martina Hingis" can be created by defining criteria on features, objects, and events.

In our Tennis case study, the following events are predefined: net playing, rally, longest point, shortest point, forehand, backhand, close-up, etc. In the Formula 1 case study, we modeled by DBNs the following concepts: highlights, excited speech, start, passing, and fly-out.

Except for those concepts, the videos can be queried based on recognized superimposed text. For example in Formula 1 case study, a user can ask for the race winner, the classification in the *i*th lap, the position of a driver in the *i*th lap, relative positions of two drivers in the *i*th lap, pit stop of a specific driver, the final lap, etc. All this information is extracted from the superimposed text. To give the reader an impression, some query examples follow:

"Retrieve the video sequences showing the car of Michael Schumacher"

"Retrieve the video sequences with Michael Schumacher leading the race"

"Retrieve the video sequences where Michael Schumacher is first, and Mika Hakkinen is second"

"Retrieve the video sequences showing Barrichello in the pit stop"

"Retrieve the sequences with the race leader crossing the finish line"

"Retrieve all fly outs"...

For querying the superimposed text, an additional part of the user interface is developed. As an example, Figure 6.17 shows the query "retrieve the video sequences showing Barrichello in the pit stop".

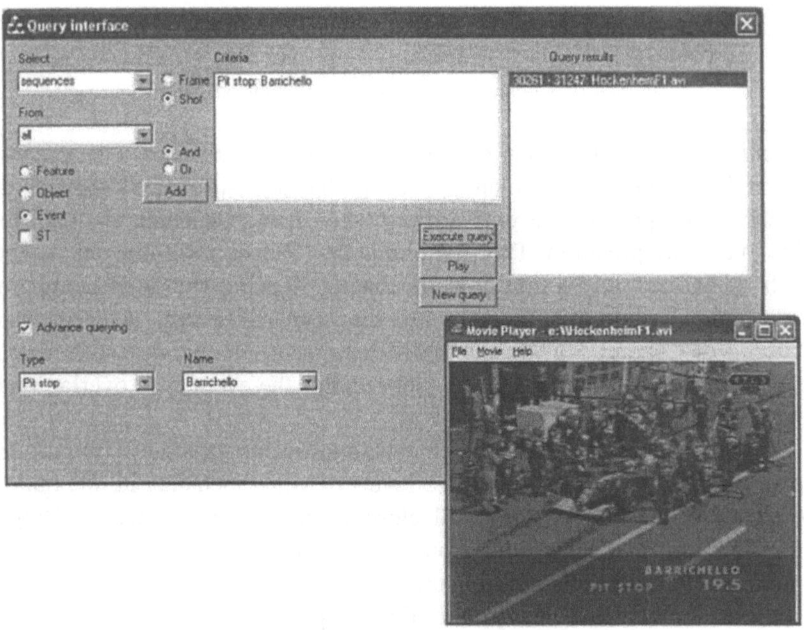

Figure 6.17. Querying based on the superimposed text

As mentioned at the beginning of this section, the system benefits of combining the results obtained from different techniques for semantic content extraction. In the following example, it combines results acquired from dynamic Bayesian networks and text recognition, and answers very detailed complex queries, such as:

"Retrieve all highlights showing the car of Michael Schumacher" (Figure 6.18),

"Retrieve all fly outs of Mika Hakkinen in this season",

"Retrieve all highlights at the pit line involving Juan Pablo Montoya"...

The system answers the query defined in Figure 6.18 by intersecting all video sequences annotated as highlights with the segments in which the text "Michael Schumacher" is superimposed in the screen as a driver signature.

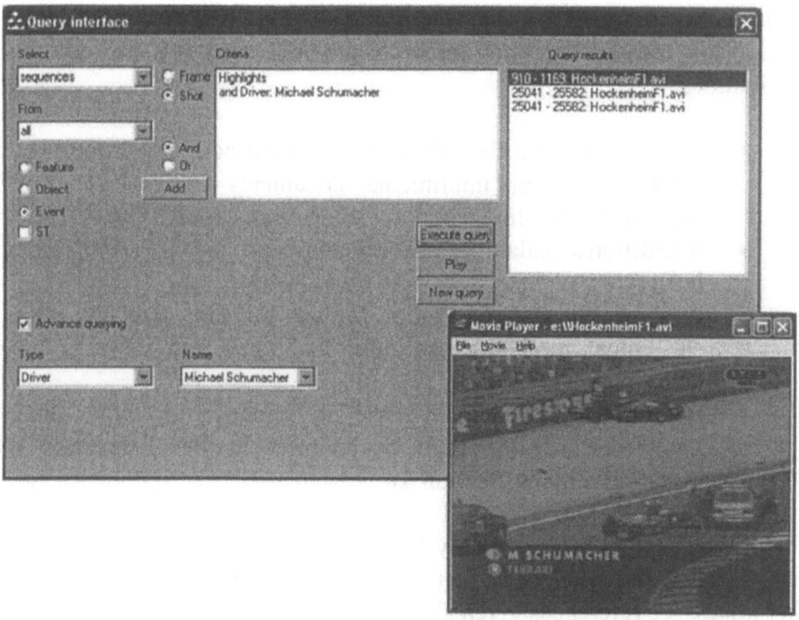

Figure 6.18. Highlights with Michael Schumacher

9. INTEGRATED CONTENT- AND CONCEPT-BASED SEARCH

Nowadays, the state of the art tools for searching information on the Web are text based search engines, such as Google and Alta Vista, or hierarchical indexes like Yahoo. They are mainly based on the textual content of web documents with very few examples that include other media, such as audio, video, and image.

Although the Cobra video framework is in the first place intended for the modeling and retrieval of video data, it can be easily extended with a domain model (schema) to provide means for searching digital libraries, intranets and the web-based collections of documents.

By extending the system with a domain schema and with methods for searching the web, a tight integration of content based video retrieval with concept based search over a document collection can be realized. In this way, video objects are treated in the exact same way as the conceptual objects of a domain.

In the remainder of this section, this integration will be explained using, as an example, a search engine developed for the Australian Open tennis tournament web site [14]. The search engine [15] combines efforts of the AMIS [16] and DMW [17] research projects, bringing the following contributions:

- It demonstrates a flexible solution for extraction and querying of meta data from multimedia documents in general (briefly explained in Section 5 and in [18] in more detail);
- It illustrates scalability and efficiency for indexing and retrieval [19];
- It shows how for a more limited domain, like an Intranet conceptual modeling can offer additional and more powerful query facilities [20];
- In the limited domain case it demonstrates how domain knowledge can be used to interpret low-level features into semantic content (Section 5).

However, in this book, we only focus on the integration of a web search method called the web-space method and the Cobra framework. For the other issues, see references given above.

The architecture of the search engine is presented in Figure 6.19. The web-space method [20] provides a way of modeling and querying a collection of web-based documents using existing database techniques. It introduces document semantics in a form of object-oriented schema, which provides a conceptual description of the content of a document collection. The web-space method is coupled with a feature grammar [8] and the Cobra video model to enable the search engine to deal with multimedia content. The feature grammars, which form the core of the Acoi system [9], describe the relationships between metadata and detectors in a set of grammar rules. For the Tennis domain, a specific feature grammar with rules that describe the execution order and dependencies between several feature, object, or event extraction algorithms is developed. The grammar is used to generate a parser which populates meta-index (see Section 5). For a more detailed description of the search engine we refer to [18].

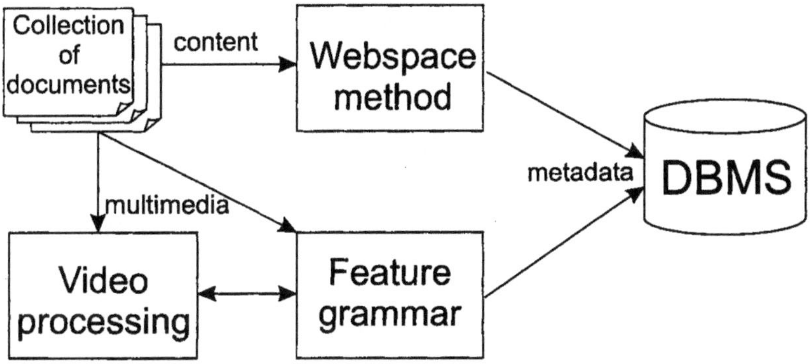

Figure 6.19. The architecture of the search engine

In order to provide the search engine with the ability to deal with multimedia aspects and integrate concept-based search over a document collection realized by the Web-space method with content-based video retrieval, the web-space schema of the Australian Open web site is integrated with the video model, as in Figure 6.20.

Given the integrated schema, one can formulate very complex queries such as: *Select the documents describing profiles of players who have been finalists or previously won the Australian Open. List video sequences of the player, which satisfies the net-playing constraint.* The more formal description of the query follows:

```
SELECT player.name, player.country, profile.birth_date, profile.play_hand
FROM profile, player, video
WHERE player.about = profile.id
AND s_contains(video, event, Appr_net_BSL:
((o1: player, o2: net),
(o1.name = player.name), (),
(y_distance (o1, o2) < 50), () )))
AND player.id = played_in.player_id
AND played_in.match_id = match.id
AND match.shows = vi.id
ORDER BY rank(player.history, {"finalist", "winner"})
STOP AFTER 10
```

However, it is very difficult for an ordinary user to create such a complex query. Therefore the system implements a graphical user interface that is used to visualize the database schema and help the user to formulate constraints and define the resulting view [21].

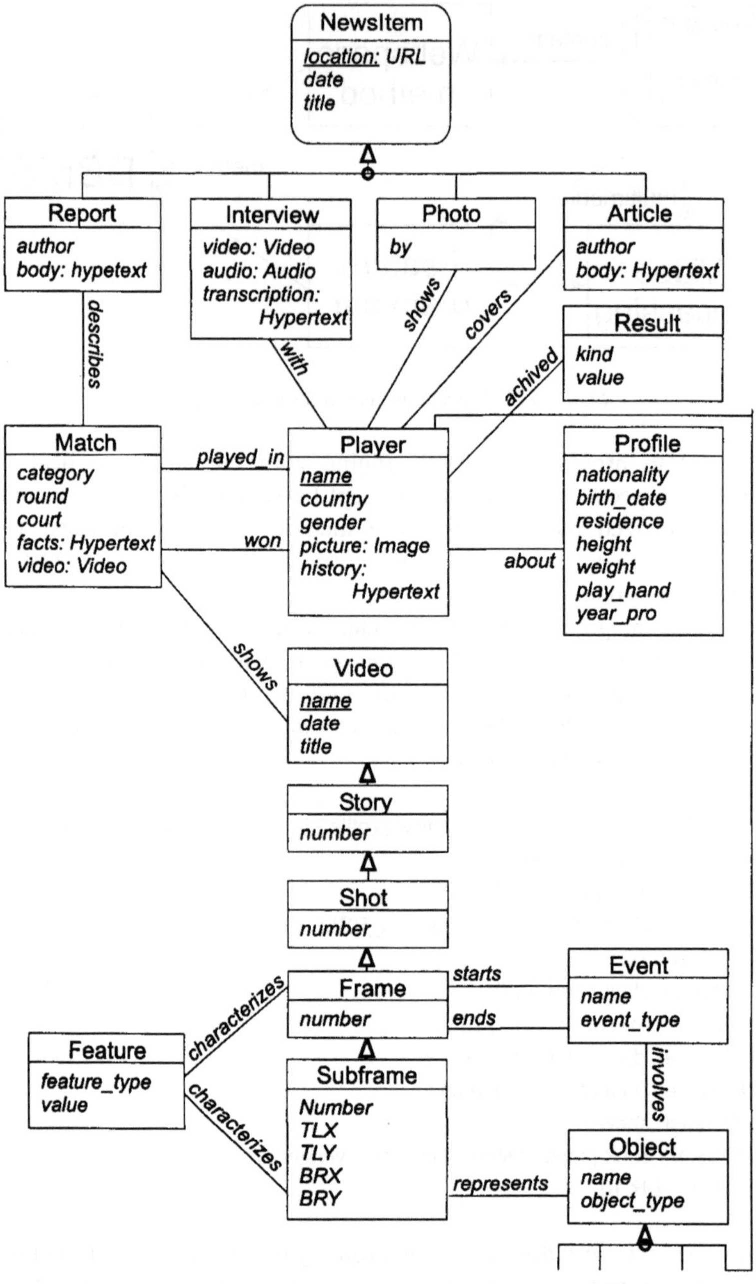

Figure 6.20. The integrated schema

The first difference of this query compared to a traditional database query is that the query information is here originally stored in different web documents. The web-space method is used to resolve this part. The part, "players who have been finalists or previously won the Australian Open", illustrates integration of text information retrieval. Actually, this part has been turned into a free text search on the words "finalist" and "winner" in the history attribute of the Player class. Finally, by defining the net-playing event, we extend the query complexity by introducing the criteria related to the video content in the same query. So, apart from querying a web-space based on its schema, the integration allows a user to query a web-based collection of documents based on their, until now, hidden multimedia content. The answer of the query is shown in Figure 6.21.

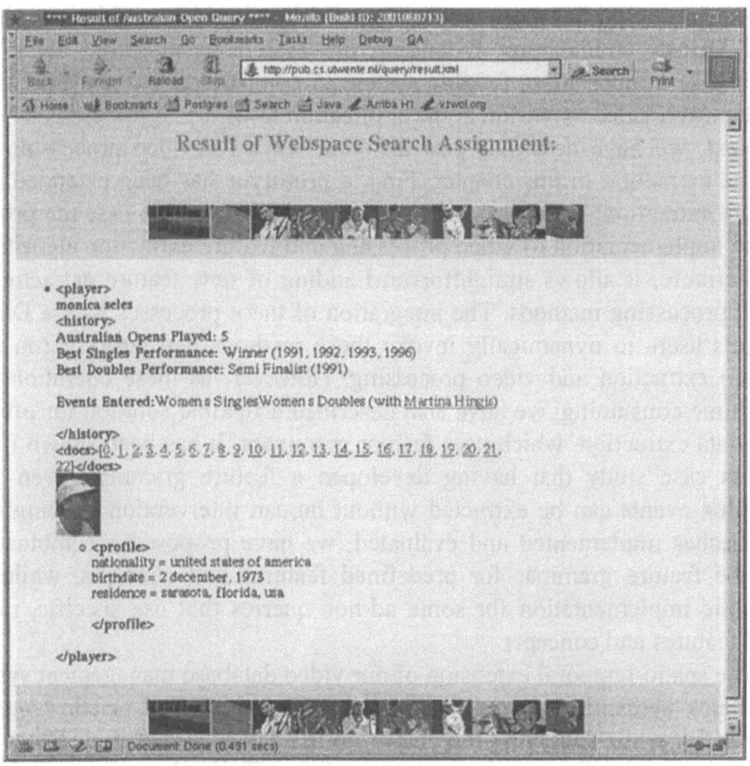

Figure 6.21. Query answer

10. SUMMARY

In this chapter, we have presented the prototype of a video database management system. The prototype implements different approaches for content-based video retrieval in a database environment.

The prototype is based on a flexible architecture, which allows the use of different techniques for feature/semantics extraction. Furthermore, thanks to its domain independent architecture, the prototype can be used in different domains. It is easily extensible for new feature extractors, as well as for new methods for identifying the video semantics. Finally, the architecture allows distributed query processing, which can considerably decrease the time needed for costly video processing and semantic content extraction operations.

The prototype has been implemented following the well-known three-level DBMS architecture. Extending the system at all three levels has resulted in a much more flexible system in comparison to the systems that implement a video extension at the application level.

Next, we have described two different ways for video processing and feature extraction in this chapter. First, a prototype has been extended with feature extraction. It uses a Matlab server in the backend to ease the process of the implementation of video processing and feature extraction algorithms. Furthermore, it allows straightforward adding of new feature extractors or video processing methods. The integration of these processes with a DBMS permits users to dynamically invoke these methods and perform run time feature extraction and video processing. However, as these operations are very time-consuming, we have also described a flexible solution for off-line metadata extraction, which uses feature grammars. It has been shown in the Tennis case study that having developed a feature grammar, even very complex events can be extracted without human intervention. Having both approaches implemented and evaluated, we have proposed a combination, i.e. the feature grammar for predefined features and concepts, while the dynamic implementation for some ad-hoc queries that use specific, rarely used features and concepts.

The spatio-temporal extension of our video database management system facilitates semantic queries that involve definitions of spatio-temporal events. So, while retrieving the data from the database, a user does not rely only on predefined annotation, which is done off-line, but can dynamically formalize some events using spatio-temporal relations and retrieve them in run time. The query processing has been explained using the net-playing query example.

Another method for semantics extraction, which has been integrated into the system, is based on hidden Markov models. It allows a user to interactively train models and evaluate them against the data in the database. For the Tennis case study, we have implemented a parallel evaluation of six HMMs (one for each type of stroke we recognize). This has illustrated how the parallelism of the database kernel has been exploited to accelerate the pretty costly HMM operations.

For the computation with respect to dynamic Bayesian networks, we have used algorithms implemented within Matlab. Consequently, they have been integrated with the system using the Matlab server and the interface developed for video processing and feature extraction extension.

In this chapter, we have demonstrated one of the major advantages of the Cobra video framework, which is the support for the integrated querying by combining different techniques for the extraction of semantic content. The system provides a user with the ability to employ all techniques presented in this book in an integrated way. While querying the database, he can combine features, objects, and events, but also the methods for their extraction. Therefore, the same query can comprise spatio-temporal formalization of a 'deterministic' event, but also an HMM extraction method for a 'more stochastic' event. This is an important advantage over other existing approaches that stick to only one technique for content extraction. In this chapter, the semantic gap problem has been addressed from the database point of view, allowing users to dynamically create and define new multimedia objects and events using different techniques.

Finally, the last section of the chapter has shown a bigger picture of the use of our system. It has illustrated only one application of the system. Here, the system has been integrated with the web-space method, the feature grammar, and a text retrieval method to support scalable and efficient digital library search. The combined efforts have resulted in a search engine that provides a flexible solution for extraction and querying of metadata from multimedia documents. It illustrates scalability and efficiency for retrieval, and increases precision in answering more complex queries from a limited domain thanks to the web-space method. Moreover, the search engine has demonstrated the benefits of combining content-based video retrieval with the concept-based search over a document collection. In this way, web documents can be queried in the database way, including their multimedia content. As a result, users are provided with ability to specify their information need in very detailed manner, and query text, audio, and video in the exact same way.

REFERENCES

[1] W. Grosky, "Managing Multimedia Information in Database Systems", *Communications of the ACM*, 40(12), 1997, pp. 73-80.

[2] A. Yoshitaka, T. Ichikawa, "A Survey on Content-Based Retrieval for Multimedia Databases", *IEEE Transactions on Knowledge and Data Engineering*, 11(1), 1999, pp. 81-93.

[3] A. Del Bimbo, *Visual Information Retrieval*, Morgan Kaufmann, San Francisco, California, 1999.

[4] W. Al-Khatib, Y. Day, A. Ghafoor, P. Berra, "Semantic Modeling and Knowledge Representation in Multimedia Databases", *IEEE Transactions on Knowledge and Data Engineering*, 11(1), 1999, pp. 64-80.

[5] M. Petkovic, W. Jonker, V. Mihajlovic, "Extending a DBMS to Support Content-Based Video Retrieval: A Formula 1 Case Study", *XML-Based Data Management and Multimedia Engineering – EDBT*, A.B. Chaudhri, R. Unland, C. Djeraba, W. Lindner (Eds.), 2002 LNCS 2490, Springer Verlag, 2002, pp. 318-341.

[6] P. Bonz, A.N. Wilschut, M.L. Kersten, "Flattering an objects algebra to provide performance", In *Proc. of the IEEE ICDE*, Orlando, 1998, pp. 568-577.

[7] P. Boncz, M.L. Kersten, Monet: "An Impressionist Sketch of an Advanced Database System", *Basque International Workshop on Information Technology*, San Sebastian, 1995.

[8] A. R. Schmidt, M. A. Windhouwer, and M. L. Kersten, "Feature Grammars", In *Proceedings of the International Conference on Systems Analysis and Synthesis*, Orlando, FL, USA, 1999.

[9] M. A. Windhouwer, A. R. Schmidt, M. L. Kersten, "Acoi: A System for Indexing Multimedia objects", In *Proceedings of International workshop on Information Integration and Web-based Applications and Services*, Indonesia, November 1999.

[10] P. Linz, *An Introduction to Formal Languages and Automata*, second edition, Jones and Barlett Publications, 1997.

[11] M. Petkovic, R. Zwol, H. E. Blok, W. Jonker, P. M. G. Apers, M. Windhouwer, M. Kersten, "Content-based Video Indexing for the Support of Digital Library Search", In *Proc. of the 18th IEEE International Conference on Data Engineering (ICDE)*, San Jose, USA, February 2002.

[12] L. R. Rabiner, B.H. Juang, "An Introduction to Hidden Markov Models", *IEEE ASSP Magazine*, January 1986.

[13] M.Petkovic, W. Jonker, "Content-based Video Retrieval by Integrating Spatio-Temporal and Stochastic Recognition of Events", In *the Proceedings of the IEEE Workshop on Detection and Recognition of Events in Video*, Vancouver, 2001, pp. 75-82.

[14] Tennis Australia, Australian Open tennis tournament – grand slam tennis – official site by IBM, http://www.ausopen.org , January 2001.

[15] H. E. Blok, M. Windhouwer, R. Zwol, M. Petkovic, P. M. G. Apers, M. Kersten, W. Jonker, "Flexible and Scalable Digital Library Search", In *Proc. of the 27th International Conference on Very Large Databases*, Roma, Italy, September 2001, pp. 705-706.

[16] Advanced Multimedia Indexing and Searching (AMIS), The Netherlands Foundation for Scientific Research grant no. 612-21-201.

[17] P. G. M. Apers, M. L. Kersten, *DMW: Digital Media Warehouse Systems*, Technical Report, Telemetics Institute, Enschede, the Netherlands, June 1998.

[18] M. A. Windhouwer, R. van Zwol, A. R. Schmidt, M. Petkovic, and H. E. Blok, "Flexible and scalable digital library search", In *Web-enabled Systems Integration: Challenges and*

Practices, (Ajantha Dahanayake and Waltraud Gerhardt,eds.), Idea Group Publishing, Hershey, Pennsylvania, USA, 2002.

[19] H.E. Blok, *Database Optimization Aspects for Information Retrieval*, Ph.D. thesis, Twente University Press, April 2002.

[20] R. van Zwol, P. G. M. Apers, "The Webspace Method: On the Integration of the Database Technology with Information Retrieval" In *Proceedings of the Conference of Information and Knowledge Management (CIKM'00)*, Washington D.C., 2000.

[21] Roelof van Zwol, *Modelling and searching web-based document collections*, Ph.D. Thesis, Enschede, The Netherlands, 2002.

Chapter 7

CONCLUSIONS

1. SUMMARY AND CONCLUSIONS

The goal of this book as posed in Chapter 1 is to investigate what techniques are necessary to be added to a database management system to support content-based video retrieval. The research that has been done to accomplish this goal is positioned at the crossroads among many fields that include among others databases, information retrieval, computer vision, image processing, and pattern recognition. All these research communities have identified the problem of bridging the semantic gap as the major problem in content-based video retrieval. In this book, we have demonstrated that the semantic gap can be closed in restricted domains by the integrated use of the spatio-tempoal approach, HMMs, and DBNs. Another major contribution of the work presented in the book is the integration of these technologies within the DBMS, which allows the system to be used in multiple domains with minimal adjustments and provides a user with dynamic feature and semantics extraction.

The following four subsections bring summaries and conclusions addressing the particular problems of bridging the semantic gap and the additional issues related to video modeling, and system architecture.

1.1 Video modeling

In Chapter 3, we have identified differences between multimedia modeling and traditional data modeling considering the requirements of content-based video retrieval. Particularly, a distinction has been made between the modeling of the video structure and the modeling of the video content, which is necessary for content-based retrieval.

After reviewing the existing approaches, two main groups of models that are concerned with the modeling of the video content have been identified: feature-based models and annotation-based models. The feature-based models use automatically extracted features to represent the video content, but they do not provide semantic representation, which is most important for users. On the other hand, the annotation-based models provide the semantic representation, but lack its automatic derivation. Consequently, they rely on manual annotation, which is static and subjective requiring a substantial amount of time and effort. To overcome the drawbacks of the two kinds of approaches we have proposed the Cobra video modeling framework. The contribution of the framework is twofold. Firstly, the integration of the low-level feature representation of video content with the higher level semantic representation provides a user with ability to query the video database by combining the primitives of both representations. Secondly, modeling the two different representations of video content forms the basis for research of our main goal, i.e. the support for the automatic mapping of low-level features to high-level concepts by integrating audio and video modalities.

The Cobra framework supports the use of different techniques for content derivation, which has been shown throughout this book by instantiating it using hidden Markov models, Bayesian networks, and feature grammars. This is a very important property, because different techniques perform differently in the derivation of different kinds of events. The framework is also domain independent, which has been demonstrated in the book by its successful application in various domains.

Finally, the framework has been extended with necessary structures and operations to support formalization of video content using spatio-temporal and feature operators. The selected spatial and temporal operators have shown to be expressive enough to formalize a wide range of video events that involve transitions of object positions and extent. These relations have provided the basis for the spatio-temporal extension of the framework, which is used as one of the techniques for bridging the semantic gap.

1.2 Bridging the semantic gap

The main topic of this book was how to bridge the gap between the low-level features and high-level video concepts. Beside the Cobra framework, which provides the basis for the research of this topic, we have identified and validated a few techniques that can be used for content-based video retrieval.

As already mentioned in the previous section, we have shown that spatio-temporal reasoning can be used in specific domains to achieve automatic extraction of video semantics. The approach has been validated using the Tennis case study in Chapter 4. First, a tennis video has been segmented into shots, which consequently have been classified in four different categories: playing, close-up, audience, and other. We have shown that simple visual features can be successfully employed to perform the classification. Furthermore, we present a robust algorithm for player detection and tracking. Finally, having the features and objects extracted, the case study has shown how the spatio-temporal and feature relations can be used to map features into high-level concepts in the tennis domain. In particular, events like net-playing, rally, and lob, have been automatically extracted from tennis videos. The formalization of events, as the descriptions of object interactions, has resulted in the easier capturing of high-level concepts of video content allowing queries that are closer to the user way of thinking (users' cognitive maps of video content).

In Chapter 5, we have focused on stochastic techniques and demonstrated how they can be successfully used to overcome the problems of 'exact' retrieval described in Chapter 4. In particular, we have centered our attention on hidden Markov models and Bayesian networks and exploited their automatic learning capabilities.

Hidden Markov models have been applied to the recognition of different tennis strokes. Consequently, the video processing approach developed for spatio-temporal formalization has been extended to achieve a finer segmentation of players shape, as well as to extract some specific shape features. Validation on real tennis data has shown that hidden Markov models can be successfully used for content-based video retrieval. We have carried out a series of experiments in order to find which combination of features gives the best result for stroke recognition. The results have proved that specific features we introduced, such as the skeleton and the pie features are of great importance. These features have increased the number and the percentage of accurately recognizable strokes and demonstrated that our approach is promising to realize automatic statistics of tennis games.

Another technique that we have identified as useful for bridging the semantic gap is based on Bayesian networks. The approach has been validated using the Formula 1 case study. The aim of this case study was to extract the video sequences that contain Formula 1 highlights. In addition, the goal was to investigate the effectiveness of this technique for content-based video retrieval by fusing the evidence obtained from different media. We have based our analysis on the fusion of the evidence obtained from the three different information sources: audio, video, and text. Consequently, robust speech and text extraction schemes have been introduced for the audio-visual analysis of Formula 1 TV programs. Next, series of experiments have been performed to compare Bayesian and dynamic Bayesian networks for the extraction of excited speech. The dynamic networks have shown the advantage over their static opponent, which confirms the fact that temporal dependencies are very important in video documents. Furthermore, we have investigated the influence of different atemporal and temporal connections within both types of networks. The experiments have shown that the inference in Bayesian networks do not vary much with the change of atemporal connections. However, the chosen atemporal, but also temporal dependencies between the nodes of two consecutive time slices, have strong influence on the results of inference with dynamic Bayesian networks. Finally, we have demonstrated that the excited speech can be automatically extracted using the DBN that includes short time energy, pitch, pause rate, MFCC, and keyword features.

Concerning our main research objective, we have demonstrated that the three techniques, which are described above, can be effectively used to derive the semantics from raw video data. Each of these techniques has been validated and shown successful in a specific application domain.

With respect to multimodal retrieval, we have shown in the Formula 1 case study that the fusion of cues obtained from the three different media results in much better video characterization. The dynamic Bayesian network, which uses only the auditory modality to extract highlights, has shown a high precision rate but a low recall rate. The network that fuses audio and visual modalities has outperformed the audio network and detected a high percentage of all interesting segments in the race. This proves our assumption that the fusion of multimodalities will result in a more robust and accurate system. The experiments with the audio-visual DBNs have also confirmed the fact, which has been observed in the Tennis case study as well, that a good data representation in the form of specific and informative features is very important.

1.3 System architecture and implementation

In order to investigate how content derivation techniques can be implemented in a database environment, we have developed a prototype of a video database management system. The prototype supports content-based retrieval integrating the three methods for content derivation. To support spatio-temporal formalization of video events, we have implemented spatio-temporal and necessary video operators. Therefore, while retrieving the data from the database, a user does not only rely on the predefined annotation, which is done off-line, but can dynamically formalize some events using spatio-temporal relations and retrieve them in run time.

Another extension implements the functionality of hidden Markov models within the prototype. We have demonstrated that this extension ensures an efficient execution of the HMM operators. Therefore, the data-intensive operations, such as feature quantization, have been implemented as MIL operations within the database kernel. Computing-intensive operations, such as the evaluation of an observation sequence, have been performed externally, allowing parallel evaluation of six HMMs on six different machines (one for each type of stroke we have recognized in the Tennis case study).

It has been shown in the book that approaches, which use domain knowledge to close the gap between low-level video features and the high-level representation of video content, are feasible. In order to relieve the process of developing systems for particular domains we have proposed an architecture of a content-based video retrieval system that minimizes the necessary adjustments of the system when the application domain changes.

The prototype has also been used to validate the architecture. Thanks to its domain independent architecture, the prototype has been successfully used in different domains. It is easily extensible with new feature extractors, as well as with new methods for identifying the video semantics.

The necessary adjustments, required when the application domain changes, include the definition of specific detectors and features for a new domain if needed, their implementation, and creation of object and events descriptions, the training of hidden Markov models or Bayesian networks. However, the introduction of a new semantic content extraction technique and its implementation is also possible.

The integration of the video processing techniques and the three approaches for semantic content extraction within the database platform have enabled dynamic feature/semantics extraction. This provides a user with the ability to interactively define and query video events, in contrast to a traditional annotation-based approach where he is enforced to use only predefined attributes. In the implementation of the feature extraction techniques within the prototype, we have taken a trade-off between efficiency and flexibility and proposed a more loosely coupled approach. It allows us to add and implement a new extraction technique more easily (for example DBNs use the interface developed for the video processing extension). The approach also allows distributed query processing using content extraction servers that sit close to raw video data.

With respect to dynamic feature extraction, the prototype uses a Matlab server within a content extraction server in backend, to ease the process of implementation of video processing and feature extraction algorithms. Furthermore, it allows straightforward adding of new feature extractors or video processing methods. However, we conclude that video processing and feature extraction are very time-consuming and that they should usually be performed off-line. Consequently, the prototype has implemented an off-line solution and proposed a combined use of the two approaches. The off-line solution dominates in extracting predefined features and concepts, while the dynamic implementation is appropriate for some ad-hoc queries that use specific, rarely used features and do not require short response time.

1.4 Overall conclusions

The research presented in the book has shown that the semantic gap can be narrowed in restricted domains. Derivation of the semantics from raw video data has been achieved by using the domain knowledge and the three knowledge-based techniques.

The three approaches, which have been identified and used for bridging the semantic gap, have each shown to be advantageous for a specific kind of problems. The spatio-temporal formalization is beneficial for the characterization of events that have spatio-temporal nature and can be described by transitions of object positions and their spatio-temporal relations (examples are net-playing and rally events). Hidden Markov models and Bayesian networks are more appropriate for events that have more 'stochastic' nature. Furthermore, by using these two techniques, we benefit of their automatic learning capabilities. Although we have not compared the two stochastic approaches with each other, our intuitive conclusion is that the Bayesian network approach is more suitable for fusing multimodalities in retrieval. We based this conclusion on the property of Bayesian networks that each feature can influence the decision with a specific probability. In our hidden Markov model approach the process of quantization, which leads to discrete HMMs, has treated all features equally. However, operations with HMMs are less time-consuming than with dynamic Bayesian networks.

We have also shown how these techniques can be integrated into a database management system. Firstly, we have achieved dynamic feature and semantics extraction by this integration. Secondly, we have improved the flexibility and generalized our approach, exploring the properties of databases as general purpose systems. Therefore, the necessary adjustments of the system, when the application domain changes, have been minimized. However, specific requirements of some other domains and possibly some other techniques for closing the semantic gap that will be beneficial in these domains still have to be explored. The next section brings some recommendations with respect to that, as well as some other ideas for further research.

2. RECOMMENDATIONS FOR FUTURE RESEARCH

The work presented in this book suggests some interesting directions for future research.

Let us start with topics that are very closely related to the experiments described in this book. As we already mentioned, we have not compared with each other the three content derivation methods. It might be worthwhile to compare the retrieval performance but also the response time of dynamic Bayesian networks and hidden Markov models in one of the two case studies we used. Some experiments are also needed to see how important the process of feature quantization in dealing with hidden Markov models is. We expect that using self-organizing maps or learning vector quantization in the process of quantization will lead to better results than the k-means algorithm.

With respect to implementation, there are some issues that need to be considered. First, it will be useful to integrate the algorithm for learning and evaluation of Bayesian networks tightly with the database kernel. As mentioned, the evaluation algorithm is very time-consuming. Therefore the methods that will speed up the algorithm are indispensable for the use of this technique for dynamic semantics extraction. Next, the proposed idea for a query preprocessor, which switches between metadata and dynamic feature/semantics extraction and performs high-level optimization of the latter, has to be implemented and validated in practice.

Although we have identified three techniques that are used to infer the high-level concepts based on low-level features, the difficulty still comes from selecting the features that describe an object or event in the best way. The three techniques, which have been presented in the book, require an expert to decide what features to use for extracting specific events. For example, in the Tennis case study, we have carried out a series of experiments to identify a feature combination that gives the best retrieval performance. The feature selection becomes even more difficult when one would try to cover metaphorical, associative, hidden, or suppressed meaning of video content. Therefore, more research concerning techniques that can automatically select the most distinguishing features is required.

Finally, very important subject for content-based video retrieval, which is only touched by this book, is the user interface and the interaction process between the user and the system. Relevance feedback is commonly used by image retrieval systems in the human computer interaction to refine the user query. Through relevance feedback, the system gathers information from the user about the relevance of features, image regions, etc. However, relevance feedback coupled with active learning is relatively unexplored area in video retrieval. Video summarization, query representation, and a multimedia query language are much related problems worth to be explored.

About the Authors

Milan Petković is a scientist in the PACMan (Processing Architectures for Content Management) group at the Philips Research in Eindhoven, the Netherlands. Before joining Philips Research, he was a research assistant in the department of Computer Science at the University of Twente, the Netherlands and a teaching assistant in the Faculty of Electrical Engineering at the University of Niš, Yugolsavia. Dr. Petković received his Dipl-Ing. and M.Sc. degrees in Computer Science from University of Niš, and a Ph.D. degree in Computer Science from University of Twente. Among his research interests are multimedia information retrieval, database systems, computer vision, video processing, content management, and digital rights management. He published a number of research articles and was invited to talk at various international conferences and workshops.

Willem Jonker studied mathematics and computer science at Groningen University. He then joined Delft University of Technology for his PhD research on knowledge-based systems. After receiving his PhD from the University of Utrecht he joined KPN Research to work on knowledge based systems, database systems, and distributed systems. In 1992 he joined the European Computer industry Research Center in Munich (ECRC, a joint research laboratory of Bull, ICL and Siemens) to work on intelligent and federated database systems. Late 1994 he returned to KPN Research to become the head of the database group and to work on applications of database technology in telecommunication systems and services. In 1999 he founded the new research department of KPN Research at the campus of Twente University. Till September 2001, he headed the department, focusing on IT infrastructures supporting multi-media content management services. In September 2001 he joined the PACMan (Processing and Architectures for

Content Management) group at Philips Research to work on secure content management in networked environments and to coordinate the cluster activities in this field. Finally, he is a part-time full professor of computer science at Twente University. Among his research interest are database systems, multi-media databases, distributed applications, content management, and DRM.

Index

MIX
Papier aus verantwortungsvollen Quellen
Paper from responsible sources
FSC® C105338

If you have any concerns about our products,
you can contact us on
ProductSafety@springernature.com

In case Publisher is established outside the EU,
the EU authorized representative is:
Springer Nature Customer Service Center GmbH
Europaplatz 3, 69115 Heidelberg, Germany

Printed by Libri Plureos GmbH
in Hamburg, Germany